The
BiG
BamBoozle

HOW YOU GET CONNED
OUT OF THE LIFE YOU WANT
AND WHAT TO DO ABOUT IT

Published by Keep It Simple Books

Cover design by Marie Denkinger
sunwheelart@earthlink.net

Books by Cheri Huber and Ashwini Narayanan

What Universe Are You Creating? Zen and the Art of Recording and Listening
I Don't Want To, I Don't Feel Like It: How Resistance Controls Your Life and What to Do about It

Books by Cheri Huber

What You Practice Is What You Have: A Guide to Having the Life You Want
There Is Nothing Wrong With You: Going Beyond Self-Hate, Rev. Ed.
The Fear Book: Facing Fear Once and for All
The Depression Book: Depression as an Opportunity for Spiritual Growth
Transform Your Life: A Year of Awareness Practice
The Key and the Name of the Key Is Willingness
Be the Person You Want to Find: Relationship and Self-Discovery
How You Do Anything Is How You Do Everything: A Workbook
Suffering Is Optional: Three Keys to Freedom and Joy
When You're Falling, Dive: Acceptance, Possibility and Freedom
That Which You Are Seeking Is Causing You to Seek
There Is Nothing Wrong With You for Teens
Nothing Happens Next: Responses to Questions about Meditation
Time-Out for Parents: A Guide to Compassionate Parenting, Rev. Ed.
Trying to Be Human: Zen Talks
Sweet Zen: Dharma Talks with Cheri Huber
Good Life: Zen Precepts Retreat with Cheri Huber
The Zen Monastery Cookbook: Stories and Recipes from a Zen Kitchen
There Are No Secrets: Zen Meditation with Cheri Huber (DVD)
Published by Keep It Simple Books

Making a Change for Good: A Guide to Compassionate Self-Discipline
Published by Shambhala Publications

How to Get from Where You Are to Where You Want to Be
Published by Hay House

Unconditional Self-Acceptance: A Do-It-Yourself Course (6 CD set)
Published by Sounds True

"Here in humble submission, in order to experience this most perfect now I deeply bow and sacrifice all thoughts, all tensions, all pressures and desires."
- The Daily Recollection

Table of Contents

Introduction 1
The Metaphor of This Book 6
A Word about the Conversation 10
The Mentor: A Different Conversation 14
The Anti-Bamboozle Device 19
How to Use This Book 22

Confessions of a Con Artist 25

The Bamboozles and Assignments
Distraction 35
Duality 47
Fear 57
Feeling Bad 71
Illusion of Control 85
Comparison 97
The Conditional 107
Collusion 117
Illusion of Separation 135
Permanence 149
Content vs. Process 165
I-llusion 175

CONclusion 189
Afterword 191

Introduction

While our books can seem (inspiringly!) repetitious, most of them have a very specific practice focus. In *The Key and the Name of the Key Is Willingness*, we explored Awareness Practice as the key to waking up and ending suffering. A bit down the road, we realized people were too mired in self-hate for "waking up" to be available. To get out of a relationship with egocentric karmic conditioning/self-hate (*There Is Nothing Wrong with You*), we began to encourage a relationship with conscious, compassionate awareness, the wisdom, love, and compassion we authentically are.

In *What You Practice Is What You Have*, the sequel to *There Is Nothing Wrong with You*, our code name for wisdom, love, and compassion is "the Mentor." We met much resistance to Recording and Listening, the tool that we developed to help create a relationship with the Mentor. So, next, in *I Don't Want To, I Don't Feel Like It: How Resistance Controls Your Life and What to Do about It*, we tackled resistance, revealing how egocentric karmic conditioning/self-hate fights to stay in control of a human life, and how we can transcend it.

Transcending resistance requires the ability to direct attention where we choose. Developing the skill of directing attention brought us to the next book, *What Universe Are You Creating?*

Through this journey we've realized there is a "meta-process" that anyone who chooses to end suffering can and must practice. That process is the subject of this book: **getting out of the conversation in the head.**

"Conversation in my head? What are you talking about?"

If this is your reaction, let us assure you it's a common one! For most people, what we call the conversation in the head is "just me thinking." It takes a bit of looking to realize that what asks the question "What are you talking about?" IS what we're talking about!

We are talking about the seemingly innocuous constant content of the mind, the thoughts that go through the head incessantly.

Everyone hears voices, whether they recognize them as voices or not.

The conversation may sound something like this:

Gosh, it's so beautiful outside. I wish I could just go for a long walk and enjoy the day. But there's so much I need to get done and precious little time to do it. I wish I weren't so busy. It would be wonderful to have time to do the things I enjoy...

Or the conversation goes something like this:

You should go for a walk. Nah, I just have way too much to do. You're going to get fatter if you don't exercise! Yeah, well, if you can figure out how I can go for a walk and get all this done.... Sheesh, my life stinks!

Perhaps you noticed that in the first example it seems as if a person is observing and commenting, whereas with the second example there's a back-and-forth involving "I" and "you." The important fact is that **it's one process.** The "voices" are what we call egocentric karmic conditioning/self-hate "talking" and creating "my reality." What the voices say maintains a sense of "who I am" and their conversation is what most of us experience as "my life."

As long as attention is captured by the conversation in conditioned mind, a person is not HERE, in the present, in the moment in which Life is actually happening. We are not living in the world as it is. We are living in a story, in an illusory reality created by the activity in conditioned mind that **appears** to be real.

Choosing to live in an illusion is not a problem, except that we suffer when we do. Dissatisfaction is the result of preferring a "reality" that is not and can never be "real." The truth is that the conversation in conditioned mind does not prepare us to be with Life as it is. Caught up in the conversation, not only do we miss our lives, we feel ill-equipped to live! For instance, many of us never come to terms with the fact that we will get sick or grow old or die. We suffer deeply when the realities of life happen to us or someone we love, and instead of preparing for the inevitable we spend an inordinate amount time and money trying to avoid it.

The Buddha taught that the root cause of suffering is ignorance of True Nature. Being tricked by egocentric karmic conditioning/self-hate to ignore what is so and attend instead to its constant conversation is how we lose connection with awareness of True Nature.

The Buddha also taught that suffering IS, and that there's a cause of suffering. Blessedly, he also gave us a path to end suffering. When we see how suffering is caused, we can choose not to entertain or perpetuate that cause.

Suffering is a predictable and universal process. In the following pages we reveal twelve of the most common ways suffering is created and maintained. When we see these "bamboozles" operating in our lives, we can practice dropping them and making the movement out of the process of suffering.

The Metaphor of This Book

Most people live in a conditioned conversation that keeps the illusion of an alternate reality **appearing** to be real. The "big bamboozle" refers to the process by which we are conned into believing and living as if the illusion is real. The confidence game is a metaphor for how we are tricked out of being present to our lives.

It is helpful to use any device to assist us in questioning what we assume to be true. The Zen saying "finger pointing at the moon" is encouragement to "look at the moon, not the finger." We want you to look at the experience the confidence game metaphor directs you toward, not the metaphor itself. We're not saying there's a literal con artist running a con game in your head, although, when we pay attention it can sure seem like it!

Here is a guide to the metaphor.

-- A con game is defined as a swindle in which the victim is persuaded to trust the swindler in some way.

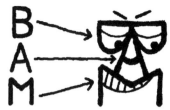

Synonyms for "swindle" are cheat, ruse, deceit, fraud, trick, deception. In this book, the "con artist" is a personification of the voices of egocentric karmic conditioning/self-hate.

-- The con is perpetrated through constant conversation in the head.

-- The conversation takes us away from HERE, away from Life as it is. It cons us into believing there is a reality other than what is unfolding in this moment.

-- The conversation creates a false sense of "me," a "someone" participating in the reality the con artist is maintaining through the conversation.

-- The ways we are conditioned to give the con job attention, and what happens as a result, are explored in the book as the tricks and bamboozles of a clever swindler.

-- The outcome of the con game is always dissatisfaction and suffering.

The exit from the con game is to see it but not believe it.

Seeing but not believing is a "gotcha" moment for us, rather than for the con artist.

One of the Buddhist sutras recounts this encounter between an awestruck Hindu priest and the Buddha.

Priest: Master, are you a god?
The Buddha: No, I am not.
Priest: Are you a celestial being?
The Buddha: No, I am not.
Priest: Are you a supernatural spirit?
The Buddha: No, I am not.
Priest: Are you a human being?
The Buddha: No, I am not.
Priest: Then what are you?
The Buddha: I am awake.

When asked what he was, the Buddha pointed us to a process. He said, "I am awake." The Buddha's definition of enlightenment is being present to Life as it is, vibrantly alive to what is unfolding in the moment and in harmony with what is so.

Not listening to the voices, not believing the conversation in the head, "seeing" that the conversation is not reality, that there is no parallel existence more real than thisherenow, is central to the practice of waking up and ending suffering. As we say in the dedication to this book, sacrificing all thoughts, all pressures, all tensions and desires is the way to experience this most perfect NOW.

It is the way out of being bamboozled.

A Word about the Conversation

The incessant conversation about an imaginary world is the con artist's primary weapon for tricking us out of the present.

Here is an illustration.

I save and save for a much-needed vacation on an island with endless white beaches and drinks with umbrellas in them. I arrive. It's gorgeous. But all I hear in my head as I walk on the beach or sip my drink is, "I can't believe you're spending all this money. This is crazy. It'll be over soon and you'll be poorer with nothing to show for it. You could have invested the money and had something for your retirement. What happens if you lose your job? The economy isn't all that good. Other younger, smarter people are hungry for your place in the company." And on and on it goes...

The only part of the story that isn't imaginary is the person not enjoying the vacation! Everything else—the job, the economy, the future, retirement, and how it could come to pass—**happened in a conversation.** Attention was on an imaginary world, and the person was conned out of an immediate experience of a walk on the beach. It's not that any of those future predictions might not come to pass; it's simply that **they are not happening right now.**

We are duped, fooled into "ignore-ance" of the present, of all that we can be and experience. After falling for some imagery scenario and then coming to, we realize we were scammed and that there was no truth in any of it.

We have to get out of the conversation!

This is a fairly simple concept to grasp, at least intellectually. "There's a conversation in my head that my attention is on 24/7. That conversation determines my relationship with myself, everyone else, and life in general. So I need to stop listening to it. Okay. Got it."

Actually, no, I haven't got it.

What I have is only an intellectual understanding. What happens in an intellectual understanding is that the con artist co-opts the message, keeps right on talking, **and we go right on listening and believing.** There isn't a blip in our devotion to the self-improvement programs we are hoodwinked into believing we need; the feeling bad for being criticized; the trying to meet the ever-changing standards of the voices; the arguing for our world view; or the defending, colluding, hiding, rationalizing, and in every way choosing the conversation over being HERE.

Thus, our practice focus is to
1) realize there is always a conversation,
2) recognize the one we're in now,
3) drop it, and
4) direct attention to the life experience we choose.

Seeing the bamboozle, we can practice a behavior change that transcends it.

Often, people are surprised that it takes concerted, focused effort to live HERE. If the present is our natural state, shouldn't being here be easy?

Well, yes, it would be if we hadn't been so thoroughly conditioned into falling for the con game. Being HERE, therefore, has to be a moment-by-moment practice, a lifelong commitment.

Fortunately, the practice is joyful!

The Mentor: A Different Conversation

Language is representational—we talk and think about things. Words represent things; words are not the things themselves. Just as the menu is not the meal, words are at a distance from the thing, much like the finger pointing at the moon.

Life, the Intelligence That Animates, the Authentic Nature of All Being, directly informs us constantly, with no gaps in the communication. When we are present, we receive Life's information through insight and intuition. Clarity comes to us directly, arriving as lucidity that the brain then translates into words.

As an everyday example, we all have remembered something important just in the nick of time. "Don't forget your umbrella," as we reach for the car door. "You left your keys on the table," as we walk out of the restaurant. We might not hear words when the information drops in, but the information drops in clearly.

Every quote we read or hear that gives us a moment of "ah ha" or "ah, yes" or "uh huh" is the experience we're talking about. For a moment we are taken out of a conditioned orientation and we glimpse the eternal. If there's anything that can be called a "Zen moment," that's it! The veil drops, the curtains part, and we catch sight of that which contains what we customarily see as reality.

If we're present for it, we realize it's a whole-body, whole-being "event." It is an experience of immediate, direct "understanding."

We all have the capacity to receive and embody the Intelligence That Animates. We can practice tuning in to innate Intelligence, the source of wisdom, love and compassion. It is, after all, what we are.

This way of being in the world is not customary. From a young age, we are taught to abandon our natural authenticity and to consult instead the ego-survival system as the authority on how to live.

In the words of Jacob Needleman, the ego, our ordinary "initiator of action" "is an ephemeral construction, which in the unenlightened state of awareness represents a kind of blockage or impediment to the interplay of fundamental cosmic forces. Because of our identification of ourselves with the ego, what we ordinarily call action, or doing, cuts us off from the complete reception of conscious energy in our bodies and actions."

In other words, identifying with the conversation in conditioned mind cuts us off from accessing the wisdom that we are authentically.

Most of us can't simply drop the conversation in conditioned mind and step into the spaciousness of the present moment because the con game is taking up all the space. A crucial step on our way to being in the moment is to learn to direct attention away from the conversation in conditioned mind and turn attention to the Mentor.

What is "so" we call thisherenow. The Mentor is the voice of thisherenow. We use "the Mentor" to point to the wisdom, love, and compassion that is the Authentic Nature of All That Is. The Mentor articulates a direct experience of Life to the authentic human incarnation present to receive it.

The Mentor is an unconditionally loving friend, the wisest of coaches. We put Authentic Being in the form of a "person" so that the experience is not nebulous, just as we put conditioning in the form of a con artist. When we're talking with the Mentor, we can **feel** the authentic nature of the relating. It's a palpable experience. It's how we experience what we truly **are** without any of the "personal" that ego is always attempting to insert.

Until we have done a good deal of Awareness Practice, our deepest and most powerful relationship is with the con artist. Now we must build a new relationship with thisherenow, with the Mentor. The new relationship is loving, compassionate, kind, and caring. The old relationship is harsh, judgmental, and punishing.

Is the relationship with the Mentor permanent? Who can say? What we know is that, as far as we can tell, it's an essential step for most people to get out of the quagmire of the con game's hateful, conniving, and wholly artificial world.

A word to the wise: If we want to speak from thisherenow, we need to let thisherenow do the speaking. To prevent us from **experiencing** the Mentor, the con artist **will** attempt to impersonate the Mentor and **will** learn Mentor language and tone of voice. **The con artist will use everything to scam us.** We can just know that.

To find out more about developing a relationship with the Mentor, we refer you to *What You Practice Is What You Have: A Guide to Having the Life You Want*.

The Anti-Bamboozle Device

"The enemy has an outpost in
my mind."
-- Sally Kempton

Like all good propagandists, the
con artist has control over the
narrative and the memory banks.
Until we begin to use the tools of Awareness
Practice to create an exit, most of what we
experience in life (after about age 7, we're told)
happens within the closed system of the con game.
In fact, every exit that is offered to us is
converted by the con artist into an on-ramp back
into the con game. For instance, we can be duped
into having a conversation about getting out of the
conversation!

Going unarmed up against such a formidable
opponent as the con artist is foolish. The best tool
we've found for getting out of the conversation
and defeating the "great bamboozler" is the
practice of Recording and Listening.

Through Recording and Listening we develop a
relationship with the wise, loving, and compassionate

Mentor. We cultivate a relationship with a reliable source of information about what is so: Life itself!

This is the best way we know to get out of the clutches of the con artist, which makes Recording and Listening practice the best way to get out of the conversation. (See what we did there? Yep, repetition.)

The practice of Recording and Listening disrupts the "con"versation. Recordings about what is true for us, what we love, what gives us joy, what we appreciate about the life we have, what we are grateful for, and so forth, begin to replace the narrative of the con artist.

**Recordings become evidence
we can count on.**

We can record the lies of the con artist, follow that with what is true, listen to our recordings often, and in this way not get fooled into forsaking the true by believing the lies. Listening to our recordings supports us in re-calibrating the attention to HERE.

Note: For more information on the nuts and bolts of Recording and Listening practice, check out *What Universe Are You Creating?*, as well as the many resources at www.recordingandlistening.org.

How to Use This Book

Most books are meant simply to be read. This book is not!

It's a workbook, a practice book, or a play book, if you prefer.

Each of the following sections describes one of twelve universal structures that keep us in the world of dissatisfaction. At the end of each section are four assignments, one for each week of the month. They provide ways to see the specific bamboozle in action and tips on outwitting the con artist.

We recommend that you read a section, Record and Listen to it, and then for a month train yourself to catch and transcend that bamboozle before moving on. This way, it is possible to practice with this book as a yearlong awareness retreat.

It is perfectly acceptable to just read the book, of course. It's also possible to do this at whatever pace you choose. But practicing with the assignments, not merely reading the book, makes it less likely that the material is reduced to more fodder for the con artist to incorporate into the conversation.

STOP A MOMENT! CHECK IN!

Did the con artist just start a campaign to get you to put the book down?

Did you hear a voice say something like...
"I don't need to do the exercises. I can get just as much from it if I don't."
"A whole year! You don't have time to do this."
"Perhaps I'll start and see if I like it."

This book is a glimpse of the con artist in action and the extent to which the conversation robs you of the freedom to choose the life you want. If all you do is watch the voices cajole, plead, resist, argue, debate, and negotiate how you work with this book (when to skip ahead, thumb past the exercises), we have done what we set out to do.

Confessions of a Con Artist

This book is about me and what I do. I am a con artist, short for confidence artist.

It might surprise you that I agreed to write an introduction to something that reveals my trade secrets. Perhaps you think that disclosing the tricks of my trade will put people on their guard and make them less susceptible to my wiles.

Not at all! I'm willing to take the risk because I have lots of evidence that explaining what I do makes not one jot of difference. How my particular con game works has been the subject of legends and myths, religions and philosophies from time immemorial. No matter how often I have been exposed, people still fall for my tricks.

So who am I, what do I do, and how do I do it?

I am called by many names. The folks who've asked

me to write this introduction refer to me as egocentric karmic conditioning/self-hate. It's a long handle but accurate. I'm often called ego or ego-I for short. It's not as accurate but it works.

Another sobriquet that flies around is conditioning or sometimes conditioned mind. My favorite is "Hungry Ghost," a phantom with an insatiable, bottomless, unappeasable appetite—now that sounds like me!

What am I hungry for? Read on...

Life is a banquet of every flavor, color, texture, sound, smell, taste, form, possibility, experience and energy. All of this is available to humans directly. But, sadly, it's not available to me directly. So, my work is hoodwinking humans out of having it all for themselves and giving it all to me! In fact, I feel most successful when a human misses out entirely on the banquet—believing life is just crumbs—while I grow fat and happy.

You could think of me as a parasite. Not having a physical body, I have to use humans to supply my sustenance. I am able to siphon my "food" (energy) from a human being through their attention. Their attention is my feeding tube.

Any person **could** just enjoy the banquet—all of it. So to prevent a person from being present to the banquet, I have to distract their attention. Through an incessant conversation, I create their reality. The world I create is one of something wrong, loss, lack, deprivation, problems, fear, anxiety, anger, hatred.... As long as I can get them to attend to my world of something wrong (with them, with life, with you) they suffer and I stay well fed.

How I do what I do
Everybody takes all of this living business seriously and personally. People think they're terribly complex and multi-faceted. They believe (because of what I tell them) that there is an infinite number of ways to get it wrong in life and everything that goes wrong is their fault. But the fact is that none of this is personal, it's not all that complex, and I need to run surprisingly few scams to fulfill my needs. (Read the rest of the book for the details. These authors reveal twelve of my biggies.)

Let me illustrate the simplicity of it all with an example of the "bamboozle" I use most often. It works every single time. I've found that the fastest, easiest way to get attention from a human is to make them feel bad. It is so easy to do! Makes one think of taking candy from a baby.

Here's how it goes.
First, I direct their attention to an opportunity or a decision that needs to be made.

Next, I start an endless conversation on either side of the decision to be made. Should I this, or should I that? Jumping from one side to the other. Back and forth.

Should I stay in this job or find another?
Do I like this or not?
Make the call now or later?
Pursue this relationship or let it go?
Invest the money or go on vacation?
Did this go well or did it not?
Do they like me or do they not?
Stop on the way to work and get coffee or not?

Then, time runs out and I force them to take action. This is where it gets really fun because the human does not know that **there is no way to get it right.** I twist whatever they do as a "mistake." I tell them that whatever action they took was the wrong one. Just a hint, a little word, sometimes a twinge, a funny sensation, and off they go! I've trained them so well! Panic sets in and they look to me to get out of the situation that I just bamboozled them into! (Oh, joy!) Helpfully, I let them know there is nothing they can do. It's a mess. It's their fault. Just like all the other times. And, poof! They feel bad! Well, miserable, actually. They fall for it every single time!

I just sit back, watch their energy tank as I gobble it up, and enjoy my banquet!

But, of course, I don't let them go on feeling bad for very long, just until I've had my fill. And then I set to work on the next setup, the next con, the next buildup of energy—my next feast.

Let me say that I am not actually all that greedy. Much of the time I keep people on a maintenance program of low level energy transfer. In maintenance, nothing big is happening. The person has no idea they are being bamboozled or that I have their attention. From their perspective, everything is normal. My voice is just droning on in the background. But, since I do like a feast now and again, I orchestrate periodic forays into real suffering drama.

My system is foolproof. The best thing I have going for me is that I can convince human beings that we are one and the same—they are me and I am them. Stop and take that in for a moment! Once humans believe that lie, they will argue for me, believe me, trust me, defend me, hide me, and, above all, choose me. In fact, they identify with me to such an extent that they have no experience of what they really are (and even when they do, they can't believe it). The whole thing results in a life of dissatisfaction for them and all of their energy for me.

And here is the kicker: once someone is in relationship with me, they become addicted. They want to give all of their attention to me because they so deeply believe they **are** me. The ones that try to end a relationship with me usually find it so difficult and painful they quickly give up.

I am not saying that I am always successful or that humans have no choice. It's a game, after all, and humans do have the capacity to wake up and end my little reign of supremacy whenever they choose. That would not be my choice, obviously, and I do put up a vicious fight, but it is how the game is played, and I pride myself on being philosophical about it. I know I'll have many more chances to turn the situation to my advantage. For instance, one of my slickest tactics is to jump on board the end-the-reign-of-supremacy-and-take-back-my-life train. "Yes! Let's show it who's boss! Let's claim our power!" Makes me smile just thinking about it.

My motivation to reveal my playbook is to add a little spice to the game. I enjoy being challenged. This is the opening gambit.

See if you can spot me as I bamboozle you.

Let the games begin.

The Twelve Bamboozles and Assignments

BAMBOOZLE NO. 1

This little cartoon introduces Ego Bamboozle No. 1: DISTRACTION.

The way this bamboozle often plays out in meditation can go something like this:

It's time to meditate. It's what I want to do. I sit down to meditate. Three breaths in and the conversation starts:

"You didn't fold the laundry."
"If you don't send that email now you'll forget."
"How long has it been since you called your mother?"

35

Suddenly, a whole raft of activities that had no importance before I decided to meditate **have to be done right NOW.** Attention goes to my to-do list, plans, problems, schedules, demands—all essential to do **now.** I cease to be present for the only time that exists—this very moment. By the time the meditation period ends, I have written a presentation, laid out the week's plan, and composed several emails. There was no meditation; I just spent 30 minutes noodling around in conditioned mind.

Like a magician performing sleight of hand, the con artist constantly directs our attention with, "Look! Over there," training us to attend to **anything** other than thisherenow. We're bamboozled into believing something is more important than being present where we are. We can't have what we seek, not because it is not HERE, but because we are distracted from receiving it. In reality, everything we are seeking is HERE, **but we are not.**

The distraction bamboozle is life or death for egocentric karmic conditioning/self-hate. The con completely and desperately depends on the attention it can grab because any time we aren't falling for its yammering its illusory existence ceases altogether.

When we bring attention to the present, we see various manifestations of distraction playing out.

Productivity

Ever wonder why multi-tasking gets so much buzz? "You'll get a lot more done," goes the hype, "if you do several things simultaneously." The truth is we can only attend to one thing at a time. The real result of multi-tasking is feeling scattered and unfocused, wholeness replaced by fractured overwhelm. We may **feel** we're accomplishing a lot, but when we stop to look we realize "harried" does not equal "achieving."

Entertainment

Here is a particularly pernicious one! We've been trained to see distraction as entertainment, enjoyment, relaxation, and reward for having worked hard. But all that happens in distraction, whether we call it entertainment or not, is that we're lulled into unconsciousness. When we are unconscious, egocentric karmic conditioning/self-hate not only gets to snack on our energy without interruption, it gets to rest up. It doesn't have to work so hard to maintain itself, since the entertainment is doing the work of keeping the attention away from the present.

Boredom

We're heavily conditioned to fear boredom. People will do just about anything to avoid feeling bored. But what **is** boredom? Boredom/bored/boring just means nothing is happening, right? Why is that so threatening? Because, when nothing is reflecting the ego, when the attention is with thisherenow, **the ego does not exist.**

Egocentric karmic conditioning/self-hate would not be well served if it were to scream, "You're not giving me attention! I can't siphon off your life force! If you don't attend to me soon I'll die!" Instead it just says BOOORIIING, and we're trained to panic and get busy feeding it.

If this seems extreme, the next time you're bored turn attention to the breath, sit still, and just watch. Things will heat up quickly. Just sitting and watching is very much like meditation, and according to egocentric karmic conditioning/self-hate meditation is one of the most boring things a person can do!

When boredom looms, we are sidetracked into "doing something" that puts ego squarely back in the spotlight. We experience the sensations we label boredom, and we obediently turn to conditioned mind and ask, "What should I do?" "Well," it says, "check your email, send a text, call someone, turn on some music, watch tv, have a drink, get a snack...." Anything to divert us from becoming aware of the scam it's running to keep us out of conscious compassionate awareness.

Avoidance

We have been deeply conditioned to fear our feelings. Alcohol, drugs, television, food, sex, and even exercise are some of the most popular ways to avoid feeling. We're told the present will be unpleasant, even painful. The fear, supposedly, is that if we're **here**, we'll feel things we don't want to feel and won't be able to stand it. There will be thoughts we don't want to have—bad memories, images that will leave us afraid and anxious. Better to escape than to risk being present for the unbearable.

Avoiding the present, Life as it is, puts us in a very narrow "comfort zone." Without scrutiny we assume this narrow comfort zone is protecting us from the discomforts of life. But with a little observing we realize that the comfort zone is for ego's comfort, and staying with it is an attempt to avoid setting off the voices of self-hate. If we agree not to be present to Life, if we're willing to be a low-level maintenance system for the insatiable ego, we just might escape a higher level of abuse. The result is atrophy of the ability to be present to Life and authentic connection.

In restaurants, walking down the street, in cars at stoplights, and even riding bicycles, people increasingly have their eyes glued to the tiny screen of a phone. Completely focused on the device occupying the attention, we are oblivious to what's going on around us.

Without conscious awareness, the disconnect can be so complete that we go through our days resentful that life is constantly interfering with what "I" want to do. I make plans, life interrupts, and I live in frustration that my program is thwarted. We have lost sight of the fact that our life belongs to Life. We are expressions of Life; we are not the authors of Life!

Blaise Pascal captured perfectly the magnitude of the scam when he said, "All of humanity's problems stem from man's inability to sit quietly in a room alone."

The distraction scam is so much a part of our lives we don't even notice it.

-- We don't realize how often we're tricked into abandoning ourselves to the cruel, punishing process.
-- We don't see it as something controlling us.
-- We don't realize giving our attention to the voices is how the scam works.

We fall for the ruse and accept the beating when what we did is pointed out by the voices of self-hate. "All you do is waste time." "Why can't you stick to anything?" "You just don't have any will power." "You're not able to follow through on anything."

Well, actually, we do follow through **consistently**—we continue to allow the con artist to hoodwink us time and time again, without awareness or protest.

A chicken can be hypnotized by putting its beak on the ground and drawing a line from the beak out some distance. Once the bird enters a trance-like state, it will stay that way from a few seconds to half an hour or so. That's an apt image for a distracted human being. Distraction is tunnel vision. Attention is grabbed, turned to some specific piece of content, and there it stays. And there we stay, in a trance-like state, until something, usually another distraction, grabs the attention.

Turning attention away from the conversation in conditioned mind and ceasing to be distracted by its gyrations is an essential skill in Awareness Practice. We practice paying attention, learning to direct the attention, and learning to live in thisherenow. As we let go the con artist's bamboozles siphoning off our life force, awareness expands to contain all of life—all moods, all flavors, all frequencies. We get to be HERE to receive it. We get to be ALIVE.

Distraction Assignment: Week One

Set aside 10 minutes each day this week to sit quietly and do NOTHING! Watch how the con artist attempts to get your attention. What fantasies, plans, fears, stories, etc., does it use to lure you out of the moment?

At the end of each day, make a recording that assists you to remember how the con artist uses distraction to get your attention.

Distraction Assignment: Week Two

The con artist persuades us that multi-tasking is a great way to get lots of things done. Prove the con artist wrong. This week set aside a period of time each day to practice giving your attention to doing just one thing at a time.

Example:
If you usually read a book while you eat, just eat.
If you listen to the radio while you drive; turn off the radio and focus on driving.
If you listen to music and work out, just listen to music or just work out.

At the end of each day, record the benefits of giving attention to one thing.

Distraction Assignment: Week Three

This week practice keeping Life energy for you instead of feeding ego. Notice how the con artist uses "entertainment" to distract the attention. Do something that keeps you HERE, in the present rather than indulging the distraction.

Example:
I sit down to check my email before I go to bed. I end up surfing the internet and go to bed late.

Practice: I sit quietly for 10 minutes before going to bed and don't check my email.

 At the end of each day, record the benefits of choosing presence over distraction. And listen to it regularly!

Distraction Assignment: Week Four

Bust the distraction bamboozle by practicing redirecting the attention to thisherenow. Set alarms for three times during each day of this week. When the timer goes off, notice the conversation that you were attending to in your head. Smile as you shout "gotcha!" Bring the attention to the breath, pick up your recording device and talk about what is HERE. Describe the feeling of being in the body, what you see, hear and smell.

At the end of each day listen to your recordings of being HERE.

BAMBOOZLE NO. 2

"To be or not to be: that is the question."

In this well-known line from Shakespeare's *Hamlet*, the Prince is questioning whether to live or to die. For our purposes, it illustrates the next universal structure we will explore: Ego Bamboozle No. 2: DUALITY.

So what is duality and what part does it play in the ego-maintaining con game?

The dictionary defines duality as "two-fold, a classification into two opposed parts or sub-classes." Dark/light, good/evil, inside/outside, life/death, ugly/beautiful, happy/sad, left/right, and up/down are examples of dualities.

These (supposedly) opposing forces coexist quite agreeably because, in the words of Alan Watts,

"Every explicit duality has an implicit unity. We cannot have light without dark. When we define beauty, by doing so we define its opposite. That is the structure of existence—yin and yang complementing each other in a perfect circle, each containing the seed of the other."

It is only when egocentric karmic conditioning/self-hate enters the picture (no surprises there!) that happy coexistence becomes unhappy opposition.

When we are HERE, in the moment, in Life, we experience the unity of ALL. As soon as the attention wanders to the voices of egocentric karmic conditioning/self-hate, we experience the exact opposite—disharmony, dissonance, and dissatisfaction.

This is the point of the scam after all.

This con game relies on the substitution of a single word: "OR" for "AND." When that substitution is made a whole world of isolation, separation, opposition, exclusion, and division **appears** to come into being. Instead of good and evil as a unit, as a continuum, we have good OR evil, black OR white, poor OR rich, conservative OR liberal, religion X

OR religion 4. Lines are drawn, sides are taken, positions are consolidated, identities are built and an illusory "world of opposites" is created in which I am defined by the side of the line I stand on and defend.

An "absolute" right way and an "absolute" wrong way **appear** to come into existence, and we are brainwashed into believing in the vital importance of "right"—being the right person, making the right choice, and getting everything right. The focus of the attention turns to maintaining the dividing lines and the inherent unity of Life is lost.

The wars we fight in the name of the side with which we are identified are a perfect reflection of the carnage wreaked internally by the voices of egocentric karmic conditioning/self-hate. If there is an absolute right choice, then human life becomes a struggle to be the "someone" who makes that right choice.

Our version of Hamlet's question might be more pedestrian, more along the lines of:

To eat this cookie or not to eat this cookie
To meditate or not to meditate

To leave this relationship or to stay in it
To say something or not to say something
To do the dishes or not to do the dishes
To exercise or not to exercise
To take the new job or to stay in the current one
To sign up for the retreat or not to sign up for
the retreat

However banal or profound the content of the
duality, when we're caught on the horns of the
dilemma it represents, the experience can feel as
charged, as grave, and as high-stakes as it was for
the Prince of Denmark brooding over life or death.

If we examine the suffering in any dualistic
situation, we see that it is based on a set of
beliefs and assumptions that the con artist is
devoted to our not examining:

There is a right choice to be made.
It's possible to make a mistake.
The choices being offered are the only options.
Making the wrong choice has horrible consequences
that we have to avoid because we won't be able to
stand it if our choice is wrong.
If we make a choice, we are bound to that choice
and its consequences in perpetuity.

If we were the right person, we would know which choice to make.
If we debate the pros and cons long enough we will figure out the right choice.
The solution to the problem is one side of the duality or the other.
We have the ability to control the future with our decisions.
It matters what choice we make.

And if we listen closely as the debate teams of "ego yea" and "ego nay" present their arguments on either side of the issue, we notice a few other things about the structure of a duality:

-- Being caught in a duality leaves us in a place of chronic frustration. Neither choice is a good one. It's a heads-you-lose/tails-you-lose proposition. Yet if we don't choose, we live under the vague sense of dread at an unmade decision hanging over our heads.

-- There is only the maintenance of the issue, never a resolution. As soon as we're convinced we're going to make choice A, the voices argue A is not the way to go, B is better, and the duality arises again.

-- Making a choice is not any better than not making a choice. There are voices ready to beat us about having made the wrong decision no matter what we do—or don't do!

In this way egocentric karmic conditioning/self-hate hijacks the attention and takes us away from being present in Life unfolding, away from where "to be or not to be" is never a question, away from where ALL always simply IS.

When the structure of a duality is revealed, the question that arises in conditioned mind is, "So what should I do?" Of course, that puts us right back in the duality! Through Awareness Practice we learn **dualities are never resolved; dualities are transcended.** Dropping the conversation in conditioned mind is the only way out. When we drop the conversation we are available for Life's guiding wisdom.

When love and hate are both absent
Everything becomes clear and undisguised.
- Hsin Hsin Ming

Duality Assignment: Week One

This week notice the duality debates the con artist orchestrates. See how the duality is set up around decisions and choices—trivial or important—as you go through the day. Get creative in naming them and see how often the same debate occurs throughout the week.

Examples:
Breakfast Scramble: Make a healthy breakfast or eat office doughnuts?
Gym Bug: Work out or skip it?
Family Secrets: Say what I really feel or say nothing?

 At the end of each day, record what you have seen about turning decision-making over to the con artist.

Duality Assignment: Week Two

Practice with a decision you feel you have to make. Jot down what the con artist has to say for and against the decision. If you commit to going one way, watch how you are persuaded to reconsider the other side.

Example: Should I or should I not go to that party?

Pro: You'll meet new people. You need to get out of the house more. You're becoming a recluse!

Con: Too much effort. You're tired and need an evening at home. No one will miss you. You are such a wallflower anyway. You won't enjoy it and besides you need to catch up on your laundry.

(Note the amount of time spent on debating this type of issue.)

At the end of each day, record and listen to insights and awarenesses you're having about decision-making.

Duality Assignment: Week Three

The con artist has us believe there is always a right choice and we need to listen to it debate the options so we don't make the wrong choice. This week, practice the freedom of "no mistakes." Toss a coin to decide what to do each time the voices debate the merits of one or the other side of a choice.

Record your experience of being free to make any choice, since no choice is the right choice and no choice is the wrong one.

Note: Watch out for the con artist taking over this exercise, "giving you permission" to do what does not take care of you. "If all choices are equally valid and there are no mistakes, you might as well eat junk food instead of vegetables." If there were such a thing as a mistake, listening to the voices of egocentric karmic conditioning/self-hate would be it!

At the end of each day, listen to your recordings.

Duality Assignment: Week Four

The conversation about what to do, this or that, often obscures the information that Life is offering in the moment. This week, catch the attention as it wanders into a familiar decision-making story. Bring the attention to the breath, pick up the recorder, talk about the decision, and let Life drop in a suggestion for what's next. If no information is forthcoming, just notice that. Breathe and practice patience; perhaps it's not yet time to make a decision!

At the end of each day, listen to your recordings. Record anything you notice about what you've seen.

BAMBOOZLE NO. 3

"If you want to control someone, all you have to do is to make them feel afraid." --Paul Coehlo

Introducing Ego Bamboozle No. 3: FEAR

Fear is basic and universal. We all know what it is to be afraid. A list of all we fear would fill volumes. Here are just a few.

I am afraid of death, sickness, and old age.
I am afraid of speaking in public.
I am afraid of anger.
I am afraid of heights.
I am afraid of saying something stupid.
I am afraid the traffic will be bad and I'll be late.
I am afraid of trying something new.
I am afraid of getting hurt.
I am afraid of not being accepted.
I am afraid of the future.

I am afraid of not being in control.
I am afraid that the restaurant won't be open when I get there.
I am afraid of being embarrassed.
I am afraid of losing my job.
I am afraid of being alone.
I am afraid of doing something wrong.
I am afraid of hurting someone's feelings.
I am afraid that something bad will happen to me.

However profound or banal the object of fear, whatever the intensity or nuance, "being afraid" is such a common and familiar orientation that we seldom ask "What is fear?"

When we stop to examine fear, we learn some interesting things. For example...

Question: What is the consequence of being afraid of something?
Answer: We avoid what we fear.

Question: What happens when we are afraid of saying or doing something?
Answer: We don't say or do what we are afraid of saying or doing!

It is no surprise that fear is a big weapon in the con artist's arsenal. Through a constant conversation of risk and peril, the voices of egocentric karmic conditioning/self-hate control what we explore, what we pursue, what we choose, and how we behave. By posting Danger, Do Not Enter, Wrong Way, No Trespassing signs on the areas that would expose the scam, and by convincing us those areas contain hazards we cannot face, the con artist guarantees our bondage.

We all know the quote by FDR, "The only thing we have to fear is fear itself," but it's easy to miss the magnitude of the statement. Few people know what fear is, confusing reaction to **content** (flying, death, spiders, war) with an unexamined **process**.

What we call fear is a story, a conversation in conditioned mind that is exacerbated by sensations in the body. Without paying close attention to the process, we believe the sensations are the result of the fear, but, on closer examination, we realize sensations fuel the story of the fear.

We must employ very close scrutiny to see through the conditioned beliefs and assumptions that keep fear obscured. It is true that the same scrutiny is required to free ourselves of the tyranny of all emotions we've been taught to believe are unpleasant, unhealthy, dangerous, or painful. Fortunately, because we are working with a process, it's not necessary for us to learn new steps with each new content; the steps of the process are the same regardless of content.

For instance, I feel a fluttering sensation in the area of my stomach. I've learned to label those sensations anxiety, and I look to see what I'm anxious about. Sometimes I don't need to look far—I have that job interview this morning. But perhaps there isn't anything unusual happening. I have the fluttering sensations, I look to see what I'm anxious about and there's nothing. Does it end there? No, a story starts up about "anxious things." I may start worrying about the kids, are they okay, has something happened and I just haven't been notified? Or I think about my aging parents or what would happen if I lost my job or how much I hate my job or…. A few minutes into the story (stories) the sensations are stronger. This must mean something is really wrong. What is it? Maybe….

For many people sensations in the body go unnoticed. Suddenly I'm filled with dread and I have no idea why. I don't realize the conversation I've been unconsciously listening to in my head is producing sensations in my body that are fueling more and more frightening ideas. All the attention remains with the story, the conversation in the head. Imaginary scenarios play out one after the other, stress and tension build, coping behaviors are employed, and feeling bad and self-hate follow.

We learn to live our lives attempting to minimize, or avoid altogether, any possibility of risk. We put helmets on our toddlers, drive enormous crash-proof cars, install elaborate security systems in our homes, buy insurance for every eventuality— all in pursuit of safety.

Yet in our more lucid moments we know, deep down, that there's no such thing as safety. Despite our best efforts, what we want to happen doesn't and what we don't want to happen does. Not all the time, obviously, but often enough to keep us in a story of fear. Where does this leave us?

Blessedly, where this leaves us is right HERE! We cannot be afraid in the moment.

In the moment,
no such thing as fear exists.

Many of us have been hyper-aware and present in the face of sudden danger. The car hits an icy patch, slides toward the ditch, and we fight to stop the skid. A rattlesnake is coiled in the path as we round the curve. The plane lurches and drops, leaving our stomach at the previous altitude. The senses are heightened, the attention is focused, and all the faculties are available and engaged.

It is only **after** the danger has passed that the voices of fear start in. "My whole life flashed before my eyes!" "The entire house could have gone up in flames." "I could have been killed!"

The story is created after the fact and is embellished in the retelling.

Like all bamboozles, a story of fear robs us of our innate capacity to be with and experience all that Life is. By trying to avoid pain, grief, worry, anxiety, and loss, we close ourselves off to love, joy, peace and compassion.

Our sense of what is possible for us shrinks in proportion to what we believe we need to avoid or control. We avoid anything that threatens ego's tiny, carefully constructed universe. Our lives become pinpoints.

I don't go to parties.
I can't do that job.
I need time to prepare so don't put me on the spot.
I don't do well under pressure.
I don't like surprises.
I'm not good at that.
I'm not the kind of person who....

In the words of Alan Watts, "The desire for security and the feeling of insecurity are the same thing." As we would say it, "The desire not to be afraid and being afraid are the same thing."

In our (futile) attempts to control Life, we are trained out of living. Avoidance becomes our strategy. The desire to control circumstances and outcomes quashes the excitement, vitality and curiosity of presence.

As Kahlil Gibran wrote, "Many of us spend our whole lives running from feeling with the mistaken belief that we cannot bear the pain. But we have already borne the pain. What we have not done is feel all that we **are** beyond that pain."

When we don't fall for a story of fear, when we stay with sensations in the body and open to experiences the con artist tells us to avoid, we discover that what we are and the intensity and vitality of Life are one and the same.

When we are HERE, we are in life as it unfolds. In fact, we **are** the unfolding. Only the illusion of a someone, an ego, "outside" of Life experiences fear. Ego-identity (the con artist, egocentric karmic conditioning/self-hate) **is** fear. It is the experience of an illusory self outside of Life.

With Awareness Practice, we learn to recognize the story of fear, to stop believing ourselves to be the "someone" that is fearful, and to disconnect the story from the sensations labeled fear. Over time, we learn to re-label the sensations of dread, anxiety, and worry as curiosity, anticipation and excitement. In cultivating the capacity to stop believing we are afraid of the dark, we step into being the presence that can switch on the light and dispel the illusory monsters.

We realize the safety we're seeking is the certain conviction that Life is living us perfectly. Life **is** Intelligence. The safest place for us to be is HERE. Does being HERE mean nothing we've been conditioned to believe is "bad" will happen? Of course not. Anything can happen in Life. The difference is that we can be **with** whatever happens in conscious, compassionate awareness.

Fear Assignment: Week One

You will need a blank wall and some post-it notes for this exercise.

The con artist loves to keep us in fear and is constantly telling us what we are, or should be, afraid of. We usually don't question whether what we're told is true. This week jot down all the things you think, or are told, you're afraid of. Write each "fear" on a post-it and put it up on the wall.

At the end of each day, choose one fear to work with. Record about it; really explore it. How does that fear control you? Are you really afraid of that? Have you ever gone beyond that fear and been okay? How would your life change if you never heard that fear story again? Listen to your recording. Then make a recording about what you're seeing.

Fear Assignment: Week Two

How does the con artist use fear to control what you do? What do you avoid because you are made to feel afraid? Take some time this week to record how fear has limited what you are allowed to do in your life.

At the end of each day, record some of the possibilities available to you when you stop listening to the fear-mongering con artist.

Fear Assignment: Week Three

What would you like to hear from a wise, kind, and compassionate friend when you are about to do something that makes you anxious or afraid? Record what this person would say to reassure and encourage you. Listen to the recording.

Do this exercise at least three times this week.

Listen to the recordings of compassionate support and encouragement you made during the day.

Fear Assignment: Week Four

Challenge yourself to confront fear and prove fear is a story. Choose to do something you're told you're afraid to do. Example: I'm afraid to pay him a compliment because he might be rude to me and I can't handle the rejection.

Watch the voices ramp up to make you feel afraid. Just stay with the sensations and watch what happens; record what's going on for you—the feelings, the sensations, and the story. Listen to the recording you made and notice how your relationship to fear is changing.

Over the week, continue to practice with what the voices say you are afraid to do.

Make sure the con artist does not talk you into doing something dangerous that will harm you or someone else.

BAMBOOZLE NO. 4

"When before the beauty of a sunset or of a mountain you pause and exclaim, 'Ah,' you are participating in divinity."
--the Upanishads, ancient Hindu text

"Such a moment of participation involves a realization of the wonder and sheer beauty of existence. People living in the world of nature experience such moments every day. They live in the recognition of something there that is much greater than the 'human' dimension."
--Joseph Campbell

"The ego is a veil between the human and the divine." --Rumi

Participating in divinity, experiencing True Nature, recognizing the Intelligence That Animates, knowing God, is available to all of us. In moments of presence we feel the awe, the majesty, and the joy of existence and our part in it. The veil drops and we realize what IS is radiantly HERE.

Presence ends the con game and puts the con artist out of business. When we are HERE, there's no time, space, or attention left over to feed the insatiable desires of the Hungry Ghost (aka the con artist). For this simple reason, the con artist employs extreme measures to combat the power of presence.

What better way to convince us that we are not divine than constantly to feed us the opposite: that we are unworthy, flawed, undeserving, deficient, and inadequate. The broadcast has to be continuous because if it weren't there would be an opening for an "ah" moment of presence that would be disastrous to the ego-identity's survival scheme!

Introducing Ego Bamboozle No. 4: FEELING BAD

Here are some one-liners the con artist uses while operating the Feeling Bad bamboozle. When we bring attention to the messages, we can hear how hateful they are.

Wow. That was stupid of you!
You are so inept!
You should have known better.
Why do I keep making the same mistakes?
How could you have done that to her?
There you go again. You never keep your
commitments.
I am such a loser!
You are so judgmental.
Oh, no. I can't believe I said that.

Whether they are "I" voices—I am such a loser!—
or "you" voices—that was stupid of you—the
message is unmistakable. Whatever happened,
there is something wrong with "me." I deserve the
reproach, I should be chastised, and I should feel
bad.

To be clear, the feeling bad we're exploring is not
the authentic, momentary disappointment at having
spoken or behaved in a way that is not in keeping
with the heart. The feeling bad we're talking about
is always the result of a conversation inside our
own head.

Here is an example of how the conversation might unfold...

"You have so much to do! Maybe you should work through your lunch break."
I work through my lunch break.

"Good grief, it's going on six already. Oh, what difference does it make? One more hour and I'll have this presentation locked up. The gym is going to have to wait."
I skip the gym.

"I'm too tired to go to the store. I'll just make do with what I have at home or grab something on the way."
I don't go to the store.

"I know eating fast food isn't good, but it's been such a long day."
I stop at a fast food dive.

Then it starts. "I can't believe you ate that! What's wrong with you? All those calories! You're going to get even fatter and less healthy! You just don't know how to take care of yourself. You skip the gym, you don't eat healthy food, you work too hard! You never learn, do you?"

We're talked into unconscious behaviors, chastised for doing what we decided not to do, blamed for those behaviors and left believing "it's all my fault."

Sometimes, for variety, the focus of attention is redirected to blaming someone else.

"Well, if my boss weren't such an unconscious drill sergeant, I could have done this presentation in a less pressured way! It's this job. The hours are killing me"

We are bamboozled into accepting the blame, or assigning the blame to someone else, and the true culprit, the one orchestrating events leading to "feeling bad," is never revealed. This is a masterful deflection of the attention, keeping the human from seeing how the con operates. Feeling bad not only reinforces the assumption that there is something wrong with me—and with everyone and everything else—it also masks the workings of the con game.

Here's a particularly nasty aspect of the con: If in a moment of grace we slip into "participation in divinity," we are trained to look immediately back to the con artist to see whether that really happened! The answer we get? "No, that didn't happen. You're delusional." The movement of attention back to conditioning slams the door on further exploration of our experience, and we are once again right where the con artist wants us— attending to it!

Sadly, we learn to feel good about feeling bad. We hold a (conscious or unconscious) belief that feeling bad and guilty "atones for our sins" and prevents us from committing more. Across cultures, there are beliefs that punishment makes people good and keeps them good.

Bertrand Russell had this to say about such a twisted belief: "The infliction of cruelty with a good conscience is a delight to moralists. That is why they invented Hell."

People are afraid not to feel bad.

Feeling bad is so deeply ingrained the mere suggestion we can be trusted to be good, decent, fair, and appropriate is vigorously resisted. We are convinced that without constant monitoring and punishment we'll "become even worse than we already are." We're bamboozled into claiming the hateful voice of egocentric karmic conditioning/self-hate as a friend helping to keep us on the right track.

Perhaps the saddest part of the feeling bad scam is that many feel "God" is doing the judging and punishing, turning the veil between human and divine into a wall.

We are fond of saying that Awareness Practice doesn't begin until the beatings stop. Until we no longer believe we are the problem and need to be punished, we can't exit the bamboozle. And until we exit the bamboozle, we can't truly practice awareness. Awareness is never judgmental, cruel, or punishing. When we are clear what is ego protecting itself and what is Life living, we are able to choose Life.

"Chronic remorse is a most undesirable sentiment. On no account brood over your wrongdoing. Rolling in the muck is not the best way of getting clean."
-- Aldous Huxley, Brave New World

When we stop feeling bad, when we stop buying into the belief that we need to be different, we can observe how we are manipulated into saying, doing, or thinking what continues to perpetuate the cycle of feeling bad.

For example: I think of myself as a helpful sort of person, but because I take on everyone's requests for help I eventually feel overwhelmed by all I have to do. Since my identity is as someone who is helpful, I am bamboozled into rarely declining a request. So I keep taking on more and train everyone around me to keep giving me more to do. Resentment arises and pressure builds. Finally I explode, yelling at the poor person who gave me one more thing to do. Then I feel awful. The voices of egocentric karmic conditioning/self-hate beat me up for being weak, for not being able to do what people ask, for not taking care of myself, for feeling overwhelmed and resentful, for yelling, for losing it, for not being able to handle it, for being unkind to the people who are supportive of me, and on and on. I then decide to be a better person, resolving never to lose my temper again. And the cycle continues.

If I become aware of the cycle but not caught in it, I can see that the helpful behavior change is to admit when I've reached my work capacity.

Expressing what I can and cannot do would short circuit the build-up of resentment and pressure and blow a hole in the feeling bad bamboozle.

The truth is we are good, are **goodness**, and on a level below conditioning we know that. We are sincere, trying to do our best, attempting to live what we authentically are—unique expressions of Life.

Exiting the feeling bad bamboozle involves practicing not listening to or believing the hateful messages of the fraud. This goes hand-in-hand with doing our very best to practice conscious compassionate awareness **all the time while not consulting the con artist about how well we're doing!** Dropping the conversation of feeling bad greatly improves the odds that we will more often experience those "ah" moments of divine participation.

Feeling Bad Assignment: Week One

As you go about your day, track the times you feel bad. This might be a vague sensation or an explicit conversation you hear in conditioned mind along the lines of "You should not have done that!" or "I am so stupid!"

Jot down these occasions in a notebook or on a piece of paper you will carry with you.

At the end of each day, record what you've realized about the waste of time and energy feeling bad is! Listen again the next morning as you begin your day.

 At the end of the week, find the grand total of the number of times you got bamboozled into listening to a conversation about feeling bad. Don't feel bad about it! Celebrate that you caught the con artist in action that many times. Have a little party; do something special.

Feeling Bad Assignment: Week Two

Feeling bad is always the end of a set up. You're talked into doing something that's not good for you or is unskillful, and then get beaten up for doing it. That's how the con works.

This week pay attention to how you're set up. Map the process of the con game. How does it work? What is the conversation that sets you up to feel bad? What are you talked into doing that you then get blamed for?

Example: I get talked into buying something I don't need and can't afford and am berated for my lack of responsibility.

Make sure you tell your recorder the exact steps of the process of getting set up. 1) I'm distracted by a big argument I had earlier with my partner. 2) There was a lot of extra stress at my job today. 3) I'm not aware I'm feeling unloved and unappreciated. 4) Walking the two blocks to the local coffee shop, this irresistible item caught my eye. 5) Just under the radar of awareness there's a conversation along the lines of, "Oh, why not? You deserve it. You work so hard and get so little for your efforts." 6) I make the purchase and feel elated. 7) By the time I reach the sidewalk, the voices have started.

Listen to that recording often.

You'll see how repeated listening will reveal the con artist's methods when the scam starts the next time.

Feeling Bad Assignment: Week Three

Practice training yourself out of paying attention to the "feel bad" conversation. Each time you catch the conversation in progress, pick up the recorder and record all that you feel good about, what you appreciate, and what you are grateful for—right now.

 At the end of each day, listen to your recordings.

Feeling Bad Assignment: Week Four

When attention is on what is, attention can't be on a conversation about what's wrong. Create a catalog of "ah" moments that represent participating in the wonder, beauty, and awe of Life in thisherenow. Set a timer for 3 times during the day. When the timer goes off, stop and experience what is beautiful in the moment. Make a brief recording of that and listen to it often.

Example:
I love the warmth of sun on my skin.
I am grateful for that little patch of green life brightening my desk!

At the end of each day, listen to your recordings of being in the moment.

BAMBOOZLE NO. 5

One Ring to rule them all,
One Ring to find them,
One Ring to bring them all,
and in the darkness bind them.
-- *Lord of the Rings* by J.R.R Tolkien

It would seem an effective way to control people
and "in the darkness bind them" is through a Ring
of Power, but, lacking one, bamboozling people
through the power of illusion works amazingly well!
Egocentric karmic conditioning/self-hate
successfully uses the illusion of control to bind
human beings to the darkness.

Introducing Ego Bamboozle No 5: ILLUSION OF
CONTROL

Most of us assume that we are in control of our
lives (or should be). We make choices, take

actions, achieve goals, influence the course of events. After all:

I plan my day.
I schedule a vacation.
I select my partner.
I quit my job.
I move to a new city.
I paint the living room.
I sell my house.
I pay the bills.

We rarely realize planning an event is not a guarantee it will happen, or working hard at a job we love doesn't mean we get to keep it forever. Mostly, life goes on as we expect it to. And because it does, it seems like "I" am in control—until one day it doesn't.

The car stalls on the way home from the grocery store.
The traffic is heavy and I'm late for a critical meeting.
I don't get everything done on my checklist.
Project funding is suddenly suspended and I no longer have a job.
My long-time partner ends the relationship.

The stock market wipes out my savings.
I lose a loved one tragically and unexpectedly.
A close friend is diagnosed with a terminal disease.

Suddenly, we realize we have no ability to control circumstances. Something has gone wrong and we are powerless to deal with it. And the voices of egocentric karmic conditioning/self-hate are Johnny-on-the-spot with "it's all your fault."

Question: So why is egocentric karmic conditioning/self-hate, the con artist, so invested in convincing us we are in control—or should be?

Answer: **Because that's the way it keeps us from recognizing the extent of the control it exerts over us.**

As long as we are in thrall to its narrative, conditioning can freely manipulate our life force to maintain itself. (Remember, the illusion of a self separate from life, ego, requires human life force—siphoned off via human attention—to **appear** to be real.) No matter what the voices say, they care nothing for our quality of life. They will say they want us to be happy, successful, loved, accepted, and so forth, but their sole interest is grabbing our energy.

The perfect set-up for the con artist to control my life is to convince me I'm in control of my life— I make my schedule, I decide about my finances, I see to my health, I determine the nature and quality of my relationships, I do spiritual practice.... Once I'm convinced of this it can

--set up standards that can never be achieved
--criticize me for anything that is not done "perfectly"
--blame me for my "mistakes"
--beat me up for not doing things right
--torture me for failing to meet expectations, and
--torment me over what's wrong with "me" when things don't work out

In other words, if I am in charge, then everything that's wrong is my fault. I am **the perpetrator of all problems and the victim of all circumstances.**

If this portrayal feels extreme, recall a time when you decided to take better care of yourself. Perhaps you were not eating well and wanted to make more conscious choices with your diet. You looked up recipes, made a healthy menu, and stocked the refrigerator. Then the con artist in your head whispered that you were too tired or too busy to prepare nutritious meals. It talked you into eating french fries and cookies and drinking too much coffee. The diet went out the window and you felt bad because you didn't have the will power to keep the commitment.

It doesn't even occur to us to ask, "How is this happening?" We just accept the assessment that "it's my fault; I'm a failure at life."

However, on the off chance a person starts catching on to the scam, perhaps starts hearing information about other possibilities, kinder ways to live, maybe even, heaven forbid, suggestions that there's a voice in the head orchestrating the suffering, egocentric karmic conditioning/self-hate has yet another ace up its sleeve in the control department: righteous indignation.

The mere suggestion that some internal, hateful, survival system is in charge of my decisions and actions will elicit a sniff of disdain, a rolling of the eyes, and murmurs of conspiracy theorists, all leading to outright disbelief. "Oh, ok, I'm a puppet being controlled by 'dark forces.' Yeah, sure, right." We can all attest to the anger and resistance that arise when "my" control, "my" autonomy, "my" point of view, and "my" way of doing things are questioned.

That pushback is ego defense on red alert, recruiting the human to go into battle on its behalf whenever it feels threatened.

Not only is our life force feeding conditioning, it is used to defend it as well!

So, one might ask, if we don't have control how does anything get done? Aren't we responsible for our actions? If we can't control the outcome, why bother planning, setting goals, or trying to accomplish anything? With this angle of questioning the con artist skillfully moves to argue a different position. This sleight-of-hand-slipping-and-sliding prevents us from seeing past the conversation in conditioned mind, successfully obscuring the illusion of control egocentric karmic conditioning/self-hate is masterminding.

As we drop the conversation and bring attention to awareness, we witness Life living effortlessly. Not only does Life grow trees, carve canyons, and whirl planets, it is perfectly capable of washing dishes, peeling potatoes, playing soccer, and paying bills.

This is why "Thy Will Be Done" has been the rallying cry of all paths of spiritual transformation. Surrendering to Life, relinquishing "control," letting go the ego, and acknowledging that the only choice we really have is where we direct attention allows us to experience the comfort and ease of belonging to Life. We move from "I need to make life happen" to "Life is living me." And in that shift we step into true freedom.

The great Tao is like a flood.
It can flow to the left or to the right.
The myriad things depend on it for life, but it never stops.
It achieves its work, but does not take credit.
It clothes and feeds myriad things, but does not rule over them.
-- Tao Te Ching

Illusion of Control Assignment: Week One

Become an expert on the con artist's "control" conversations. What aspects of your life do you want to control? In what situations are you willing to cede control? What occasions make you feel you are not in control? How do you feel about people who are controlling? Do you like being in control? What fears do you entertain about being out of control? What do you believe will happen if you're not in control?

At the end of each day, jot down what you have seen about control. Record your insights and awarenesses.

Illusion of Control Assignment: Week Two

This week see if you can spot some of the many ways the con artist controls you through subtly making you believe you're in control. If you pay attention to what you are allowed and not allowed to do, you will be able to spot this bamboozle in action.

Examples:
I can work late tonight and skip the gym.
You can't say that! It's rude.

 At the end of each day, make a recording that motivates you to be free of the control scam.

Illusion of Control Assignment: Week Three

Take a recording device with you and pay attention to the many ways in which Life works, acts, does, and accomplishes that don't require a "someone" to be in control.

Example: Flowers bloom. Crops grow. The body breathes. The sun rises. The day ends.

At the end of the day, listen to your recordings.

Illusion of Control Assignment: Week Four

This week practice giving up "being controlled."
Each time you hear a voice telling you to do
something or telling you not to do something, stop,
take a breath and yell, "Gotcha," or smile a broad
smile, or clap your hands or do the hokey pokey or...
your choice!

At the end of each day record your
experience of being free from the
control of the con artist!

BAMBOOZLE NO. 6

"Mirror, Mirror, on the wall, who's the fairest of them all?"

Fairy tales were meant to be instructive, and this line from the Evil Queen in Snow White is a perfect encapsulation of Ego Bamboozle No. 6: COMPARISON.

Replace "fairest" with another adjective—richest, most beautiful, most successful, most mindful, worst, wisest, most considerate, unhappiest, most spiritual, most anxious, best, (add your own), and we can relate to the paranoia with which the Evil Queen asked the question.

Many of us go through life listening to a nearly constant conversation of comparison that usually ends in feeling bad. See if this sounds familiar: It should be different, it could get worse, it might get better, how wonderful it was before, how awful it is now, that's not right, something's wrong here, if I would change, you're wrong, I'm right.

The unexamined belief is that life is a contest in which we aspire to be the best but usually settle for being something less (often the worst) because the number one spot is already taken. There's an ever-changing standard that we fail to meet. There's always "someone" who is the ideal that we are not. There's a hierarchy of "special and important" that we just can't seem to get included in. When we do feel good about something we have done or contributed, the voices in the head convince us that our accomplishment wasn't really that great.

When we examine any situation that's causing suffering, we find comparison.

Why?

Because suffering is possible only through comparing two things and finding one of them unsatisfactory.

Life simply is. It's hard to imagine the pine tree turning to the oak to say, "I wish I had broad leaves," or a poppy pouting because the butterfly visited the rose. It doesn't seem that bees debate the sweetness of flowers or birds the merits of the trees they nest in. It appears that everything but human beings is too busy living to worry about what anyone else is doing!

When the attention is HERE, in the moment, everything is as right as it IS. In fact, HERE there's a delightful appreciation of similarities in form and structure—wow, look at those billions of blades of grass in that meadow—and a celebration of the differences—amazing, blue and orange dragonflies!

This is why the con artist is constantly trying to get us to attend to a story about what is NOT HERE! By comparing what is to what is not, the con artist keeps us discontented.

We don't pause to examine the con artist's comparative statements, none of which are true.

"I'm alone. Everyone else has someone"
"I wish I weren't boring."

"She's smarter than I am."
"I shouldn't be this anxious."
"You're hateful; you should be more loving."
"You're selfish; you should be more generous."
"You're ungrateful; you should be more appreciative."

Direct comparison might be easy to catch, but ego can also be subtle. As we look, we see all kinds of suffering built around comparisons.

Superiority: What an idiot! Can't see it even though it's as plain as the nose on her face!

Inferiority: C minus again! I guess you're just not as intelligent as everyone else.

Envy: Wish I had what she does. Clearly I don't!

Resentment: Why does he get to have what he wants and you don't?

Inadequacy: I just can't do this.

Shame: You are such a fake. There's nothing authentic about you!

Guilt: What have I done to deserve all this good fortune?

Complacency: If I have more than enough, I don't have to care about wasting water.

Scarcity: You don't have enough time or money to do this class.

Indifference: They're vermin; just get rid of them.

Anxiety: Will there be enough time? Last time it took 3 hours to get checked in at the airport. What if it takes longer this time?

Unkindness: What's going on with her hair? Did she lose her brush?

Self-Hate: What is wrong with you?

We're conned into abandoning the unique expression of Life we are to struggle to meet ego's fake standards of how we should be.

But those ever-changing, made-up standards can never to be met!

Believing survival depends on meeting them anyway, we strive, fail, are beaten bloody with ego's yardstick and left devastated that we've once again been compared, judged, and found wanting.

This is exactly what the con artist works to achieve!

Comparison Assignment: Week One

This week, catch the con artist being the Master of Ceremonies in a comparison contest. As you go about your daily activities, hear yourself being compared to some undefined standard and judged wanting.

Example:
You should have it together and you don't!
You are not very good at that sort of thing.
Add your own:

At the end of each day, record your strengths, the many things you do well, and the successes you had during the day.
Listen to it!

Comparison Assignment: Week Two

This week watch for the con artist pronouncing judgments on everyone else. See how the conversation constantly points out their flaws and their "mistakes" as compared to you or to some undefined standard.

Example:
She has more time than I do. That's why she can take on so much!

For extra credit, see if you can hear how you're judged for being so judgmental.

 At the end of each day, record what you appreciated or enjoyed about each person you met and listen to the recording.

Comparison Assignment: Week Three

This week see how the conversation keeps your attention on dissatisfaction with life as it is by constantly comparing what is to how it "should" be.

Example: It's too hot. My life would be so much better if I could afford to live somewhere cooler!

At the end of each day, record what you are grateful for in your life. Listen to it before you go to sleep.

Comparison Assignment: Week Four

This week, as you go about your daily activities, use comparison against the con artist! Appreciate similarities rather than focusing on differences.

Example: Wow. There are so many shades of green in nature!

When you notice differences, make a recording to celebrate Life's glorious expression of multiplicity of form.

Example: I love the different fragrances of all those flowers!

At the end of each day, listen to your recordings of the ways in which you appreciate and celebrate Life as it is. Listen to the recording again when you wake up in the morning.

BAMBOOZLE NO. 7

If X, then Y.

Not to worry! We have not wandered into algebra class. "If X, then Y, else Z" is called a conditional function or a conditional expression and is a basic syntax used in computer programming. Simply put, it tells a computer what to do. The "if X, then Y" part is a core building block of the con artist's efforts to tell us what to do!

Introducing Ego Bamboozle No. 7: THE CONDITIONAL

"Conditional" is defined as granted subject to, dependent on, contingent on, based on, determined by, limited by, controlled by, tied to requirements being met.

Here are some common examples of conditional thinking.

I just need to get control of my life. If I lose weight, give up coffee, cut back my work hours, everything will be different. That's the way to stop being so miserable.

Saving money now means I can have plenty of vacations when I retire.

When I have the right job, partner, children...then my life will be perfect.

When this project is done, then I'll be able to go to meditation, eat well, get some exercise.

Since I work long hours that promotion has to be in the bag.

If I quit this job, I might never find another one.

If I say the right things, perhaps my partner will stay with me.

If I don't say anything, at least they won't think I'm stupid.

I'm not safe if I say what I really think. So I won't.

It didn't work out this time; I just need to try harder.

I need to make money; there's safety in success.

If I lose weight, perhaps I'll have more friends.

I have to do this. My value is in what I do.

But we can't control life by meeting imaginary conditions. (In fact, we can't control life at all!) When we look at our experience, the processes we engage in (working hard, saying things perfectly, keeping quiet) seldom, if ever, result in the promised outcome (happiness, security, success, love). Bosses still get unhappy, partners still yell, banks can go belly up, jobs can be lost, loved ones might leave us.

In other words the "if X, then Y" con game works perfectly to produce suffering.

A web of unexamined beliefs is held in place through the constant conversation in our head. The most fundamental belief at the heart of the conditional bamboozle is that there is something wrong, it can be fixed, and I can fix it. We buy into the belief that love, peace, joy, happiness, and abundance are all "objects" that can be acquired or earned by doing something, by fulfilling some imaginary condition.

If our wellbeing is conditional, we're being bamboozled!

We accept without question the con artist's false premise that one process leads to another.

For instance:

When I go on vacation, I'll relax.
When I find the right partner, I'll be loved.
Having children will fulfill me.
If I work hard I'll be happy. (The process of working hard has nothing to do with the process of happiness! Ask anyone who is working hard!)

Since every bit of the process is false—that there's something wrong, that it can be fixed, that if you do X, then Y follows—failure is guaranteed.

In this way, we are firmly held on the ever-revolving wheel of suffering: from dissatisfaction to fear to desire to hope to failure to dissatisfaction to fear to desire....

As Baghwan Shree Rajneesh said:
"How does the ego live? The ego lives in the tension between what you are and what you want to be. Where does the ego get its energy? The ego feeds off our desire to be something else. You're poor and you want to be rich—the ego is absorbing energy, its life-breath. You're ignorant and you want to become one of the wise—the ego is absorbing energy. You are a wretched nobody and you want to become powerful—the ego is absorbing energy."

The result of falling for the "if x, then y" bamboozle is that we focus on an imaginary future instead of being HERE, present, in this moment, with Life. What we can have instead is the experience of Life living us, the relaxed, joyous unfolding of the universe.

Life is. No conditions attached.

The Conditional Assignment: Week One

Each day this week, play the sleuth and spy on the con artist. Eavesdrop and listen for at least one instance of the "if X, then Y" bamboozle.

Example: If I hurry up with this report, I can leave early.

At the end of each day, make a recording that reports on how untrue the conditional constructs of the con were and enjoy a good laugh!

The Conditional Assignment: Week Two

Make a list. What has the con artist convinced you are necessary conditions for wellbeing?

Examples:
I will be ok as long as I have a good job.
I need to stay in this relationship so I won't be alone.

At the end of each day, make a recording that highlights the many ways you are flourishing without meeting the phony conditions of the con game!

The Conditional Assignment: Week Three

Prove to yourself that one process does not lead to another. Choose a conditional belief, such as "doing dishes makes me cranky," and then prove to yourself that's not true.

Example: Sing and dance while you're doing dishes to prove that your happiness is not dependent on what you are doing.

At the end of each day, record reminders that you can be happy, content, joyful, loving—no conditions attached. Listen before bed and again in the morning.

The Conditional Assignment: Week Four

What if you are perfect as you are, if the moment is perfect as it is?

When the con artist starts up a conversation about what you have to do **now** to be XYZ in the future, direct your attention to the moment, and, being wholeheartedly present, receive the moment as it is. Say a quiet thank you. Notice how this alters your experience of thisherenow.

 At the end of each day, make a recording that takes you to an experience of the unconditional. The recording can be one of gratitude, what you love, what makes you happy. Listen to the recording when you finish it, and listen again when you wake up the next morning.

BAMBOOZLE NO. 8

"Hush, my dear," he said. "Don't speak so loud, or you will be overheard—and I should be ruined. I'm supposed to be a Great Wizard."

"And aren't you?" she asked.

"Not a bit of it, my dear; I'm just a common man."

"You're more than that," said the Scarecrow, in a grieved tone; "you're a humbug."

"Doesn't anyone else know you're a humbug?" asked Dorothy.

"No one knows it but you four—and myself," replied Oz. "I have fooled everyone so long that I thought I should never be found out. It was a great mistake my ever letting you into the Throne Room. Usually I will not see even my subjects, and so they believe I am something terrible."
-- *The Wonderful Wizard of Oz* by Frank L. Baum

The Wizard of Oz was a con artist extraordinaire. With a bag of tricks, props, and clever propaganda, he convinced an entire populace to live in awe and fear of him as a great and terrible wizard. For years, the people of the Emerald City accepted they had an omnipotent ruler they never saw and interacted with only as a disembodied voice. They never asked, "Why are we never allowed into the Throne Room?" Lulling, scamming, and frightening victims into not asking questions are the best ways for the con artist to keep the scam going.

Introducing Ego Bamboozle No. 8: COLLUSION

In our Zen Awareness Practice version of the Oz tale, we are residents of the Emerald City (conditioned mind) being conned by the wizard (the disembodied voices of egocentric karmic conditioning/self-hate). So completely do we believe the wizard's "reality" that we never question it—we believe what we've been programmed to believe.

Wondering what illusory reality the con artist has conjured up for you? Stop a moment and see how you "know" something is true. Unexamined beliefs and assumptions are a part of the "reality" created in conditioned mind and that prevent us from being present to the world as it is. While Emerald City looks slightly different for each of us, the glasses are universally tinted to produce a perspective of something wrong/not enough. Deeply conditioned to see through these lenses, **we don't realize we're wearing them**, which makes the bamboozle nearly foolproof.

In fact, we are so trained to choose our beliefs over our experience that even when we are graced with a moment of dropping into Life as it is, (the equivalent of a resident of Oz removing the green-tinted glasses and discovering everything is **not** green), a whispered suggestion from the con artist is all it takes for us to shove those glasses back on.

See if this is familiar:

I'm walking on the beach, my attention on the murmur of the waves and the brilliant sunset. Suddenly, I realize how grateful I am for my wonderful life. Then I hear a voice in my head say, " I wish it could always be like this. Why are these moments so few and far between? If I didn't have to work so hard…. " BAM! I'm back in the illusory world of something wrong and not enough.

A moment of presence signals extreme danger to the survival of the con. To prevent the whistle being blown on the racket, the perpetrator employs a cruel strategy.

In any swindle, the trickster appeals to 1) something the mark wants—fame, success, money, a love they think they'll never have—and 2) feelings of unworthiness, which drive the victim to agree to the scheme.

The agreement the con artist makes with us goes like this:

-- There is something wrong with you. That's why you don't have what you want.
-- Do what I say and you will have what you want.
-- You can't question or second-guess me.
-- This scheme is foolproof.
-- If it fails it's your fault.
-- Whatever the outcome, you take the credit and the blame, **but you don't say anything about this deal and I don't exist.**
-- This has to stay between us, otherwise, the world will know your dark secret—you are not as intelligent, secure, and confident as you want people to believe.

All agreements we make with the con artist, whether made consciously or unconsciously, come with a confidentiality clause. We are told secrecy protects us, but, in truth, it serves to keep the trickster safe and ensures the survival of the confidence racket itself.

Here is a slightly exaggerated example to illustrate how this might play out.

I hold a belief (because I am told there is something wrong with me) that I must give gifts to be appreciated and liked. So I buy affection with expensive gifts. Soon I can no longer afford to buy gifts.

If I entertain any thought about curtailing my gift-giving, the voices in my head tell me I will lose the approval of those important to me. "Remember, people don't like you for who you are! You will no longer be in their good graces. You can't stop giving gifts. What will people think?" I go along with the voice, keep buying pricy gifts, and slip into debt.

If I consider admitting I'm in debt and need help, the voices start in: "If you say anything everyone will know you're an idiot for not being able to manage your finances better and for believing you can buy affection through expensive gifts!"

Catch 22 -- Whatever I do, people are going to know there is something wrong with me!

Now my situation is desperate. I must keep giving gifts but I don't have the money. The voices whisper things like "You could give away that bottle of wine you were given. No one will know you didn't buy it." "Perhaps you can give away your grandmother's ring. She'll never know." I do it, act in ways that would horrify me otherwise, and become adept at covering up.

When my partner discovers the absence of the wine or the ring and starts questioning me, I prevaricate, stall, believing the voices when they scream at me not to tell. I can't admit to anything. That would be tantamount to confessing how deeply flawed I am. Not only am I not likeable as I am, but I've been financially irresponsible. On top of everything else, I'm going to lose my partner's approval. I fabricate a plausible explanation to defuse the interested inquiries.

We can see that our hapless human could have admitted to needing help, thereby escaping the slimy clutches of the con artist. However, there was so much shame, such a deep belief in imaginary character flaws, that hiding and lying seemed the only choice.

In this way the con artist ensures the collusion continues. Whatever happens, the victim takes responsibility. The shame of having been foolish enough to fall for the scam (if we don't feel shame, the voices will helpfully supply the words and pictures that will produce it) will keep us from revealing the swindle, primed for the next trick up the trickster's copious sleeves.

As the person in the above example, somewhere deep down we know that going into debt to buy gifts is not the best move. But we fall for it anyway. Why?

The collusion bamboozle works so well because we are convinced by the con artist that we genuinely prefer the deal it's offering, even though we know it's not good for us.

A simple illustration:
I have difficulty controlling my blood sugar, and I know that eating ice cream is not good for me. In fact, when I eat ice cream I feel sick. But no matter how many resolutions I make, when the craving starts (and the voice whispers how much I want that cool, creamy pleasure) I cannot resist. It's like hypnosis. I see only want what the voice offers me: the pleasure of indulging in ice cream. I can't see what will follow. I lose the awareness that soon I'll feel sick. To top it all off, if someone suggests I need help controlling my ice cream addiction, I am offended. "Don't tell me I can't have ice cream! I have plenty of control. I know it's not good for me."

In this example, the trickster reframes "help" as deprivation—I'm being denied a pleasurable experience. I'm told that I want the pleasure and I want it NOW. I have to have it. People are trying to stop me from having what it's my right to have. They will not succeed! I will sneak, hide, and lie in order to have the pleasure I crave.

Because the indulgence produces such intense pleasure, I am bamboozled into believing the promise has been fulfilled.

When I come to and see what's going on, I feel ashamed. I can't tell anyone, can't let anyone know what I'm doing. And so I hide it. I collude with the scam.

I am conditioned out of seeking assistance to stop the behavior.

Each time I give in to a sugar craving, the pleasure is more "real" to me than feeling sick from indulging.

But what's really being reinforced is the addiction to colluding with the system that has me believing I make my own decisions.

This is exactly where ego-identity wants me: addicted to the promises of the illusion, in denial of the actual experience, and defending the illusory reality, a full participant in giving my energy to egocentric karmic conditioning/ self-hate.

We can all relate to trying to kick an addiction (you might call it a "bad habit") and not being able to. Over time, the con traps us in the cycle of wanting, having, feeling unfulfilled, grasping for more, and believing being ever more addicted is just our lot in life.

The only way to get out of the collusion scam is to reveal it: report the con artist, stop taking the blame, and out the real culprit.

Communicating what the voices are doing and saying is the first step out of the process that creates and maintains suffering. Not communicating isolates us with a system that has no qualms about bleeding us dry for its benefit.

It might seem odd to say, "I ate the ice cream because the voice in my head told me to." It's likely to get us referred to the nearest psych ward! That cultural reaction lets us know how pervasive the control of egocentric karmic conditioning/self-hate is in society.

In Awareness Practice,
we fearlessly reveal the conversation
every chance we get,
not taking personally
what's being done to us.

Instead of going unconscious and letting the conditioned behavior play out, we bring conscious awareness to the process. We see what the ego identity maintenance system is saying and doing, and we train to stay with our experience rather than going along with the conversation. Instead of being the victim of the con game, we become an observer of the game, and, from that vantage point of awareness, give ourselves the freedom to make different choices.

With dedicated practice, we begin to see the longings and cravings as results of a story the voices of egocentric karmic conditioning/self-hate spin, and that when the conversation is absent, addictions dissolve. When the voices are not talking, there is no experience of "something wrong with me" that I have to fix by engaging with a trickster. Awareness Practice trains attention to be in the present, bringing the satisfaction the con artist promises but can never deliver.

ASIDE: Beware the voice that says, "Saying you were conned is relinquishing responsibility for your actions. You can just blame everything on conditioning!" Introducing a lack of responsibility into the conversation is another tactic to pull attention away from presence and toward collusion with the system. If we are distracted into a debate about irresponsibility, we are less likely to see that we can get out of the conversation, less likely to bring conscious awareness to the moment, and less likely to stop choosing that which perpetuates suffering.

Collusion Assignments: Week One

Why do you believe the Emerald City is green? How is the con artist coloring your view of reality?

This week, list some of the beliefs and assumptions defining the world view you have been conned into accepting without examination.

Examples:
"The right person thing to do is not to express my feelings."
"Good people always put others first."
"There is something wrong with me."
"I can't do this."

Put a poster up on a wall and jot down things as you see them.

At the end of the day, record your experience of seeing how the con artist fabricates an illusory reality. Listen to the recording and let go the illusion. Record what is true and listen to that.

Collusion Assignments: Week Two

Take off the green-tinted glasses this week and see if everything in Oz is really green!

Choose a belief or assumption to work with, something you have been conditioned to accept without examination.

Example:
"I am not adequate to what's happening in my life."

As you go about your daily activities this week, notice how that belief colors how you are. If this belief represents your green-tinted glasses and you're no longer required to view the world through this lens, how is your world-view different?

Record your experience of Life without conditioned beliefs and assumptions.

Collusion Assignments: Week Three

This week identify specific ways you've been persuaded to collude with the con artist. What secret pacts or non-disclosure agreements have you made that keep you in shame, dissatisfaction and suffering?

For example: My friend and I decide we are going to walk 5 miles a day 4 days a week. I'm so excited. I've wanted to do this forever. Then the campaign starts, "You're too tired. It's been a busy day at work. What you really need is to put your feet up. You can do an extra mile each day, and you'll catch up." I go along with it. I believe it. And I don't keep my commitment. I avoid admitting it to my friend as long as I can. I feel awful, bad, guilty, like a failure. When the voice in my head says "Why don't you quit, you can't do this," I give up. And worse, when my friend asks me about it, I say, "This is not the time to take this on. I don't have enough will power."

Record the incidents as if revealing the facts about a notoriously nefarious individual. Let the con artist take the heat instead of feeling like the responsible party.

Tell your story as if it happened to someone else. Here's how the recording might sound: The voices in his head started telling him what he can do, what he wants to do, what he should do, and who he is. And he went along with it. He didn't stand up for himself. The con artist, a lying, sneaky, slimy creep, focused only on his failure and humiliation. Those voices lie!

If you have trouble finding an example of collusion, it just means that the con artist has you really bamboozled. Don't be discouraged. A clue to this bamboozle is that it results in feeling bad, discouraged or disappointed in **yourself**.

Collusion Assignments: Week Four

This week, make a commitment to do something that takes care of you.

Example: Meditate 10 minutes in the morning before breakfast.

Practice keeping the commitment no matter what the voices say. Catch attempts to talk you out of doing what you have committed to. If the voices succeed in sabotaging your efforts, see how you're blamed and made to feel responsible. Notice the conversation is focused on you taking the blame, but there's no encouragement to keep the commitment or credit when you do.

Make a poster or a recording that assists you to remember how you are talked into colluding. By the end of the week, practice ignoring the wiles of the con artist and keep the commitment.

Record how it feels to be the person who keeps commitments.

BAMBOOZLE NO. 9

Luna: We both believe you by the way, that He-who-must-not-be-named is back and you fought him and the Ministry and the Prophet are conspiring against you and Dumbledore.

Harry: Thanks. Seems you are about the only ones who do.

Luna: I don't think that is true. But I suppose that's how he wants you to feel.

Harry: What do you mean?

Luna: Well, if I were "You-Know-Who," I would want you to feel cut off from everyone else, cause if it's just you alone, you are not much of a threat.
-- from the movie *Harry Potter and the Order of the Phoenix*

Safety in numbers is not just a theory. We are vulnerable when we're isolated. It is the reason the most successful predators prey on the lonely, the weak, and the frightened. The strategy of the hunter going for the easy kill is always the same. Separate the prey from the herd, cut them off from all support, pursue them to exhaustion, and the rest is easy. If the prey stays with the herd, the situation is very different. The chances of the predator failing go way up.

Introducing Ego Bamboozle No. 9: ILLUSION OF SEPARATION

Singled out, isolated, set apart, segregated, cordoned off, detached, cut off, shut away are all synonyms for separation.

At one time or another, most of us have felt alone in a hostile universe, alienated, abandoned, and disconnected. Many of us seek the spiritual path because we intuit that isolation is not our natural state. We seek the bliss of the union with the Beloved, the non-separation that the sages and mystics of the past have danced, sung and written about.

If we pay attention, we see that the sense of loneliness, the perception of "not a part of," is a bamboozle. Getting us to believe we are separate from Life is a calculated strategy to ensure the only truly intimate relationship we have is with the ego maintenance system controlling us.

Alan Watts said: "We do not 'come into' this world; we come out of it, as leaves from a tree. As the ocean 'waves,' the universe 'peoples.' Every individual is an expression of the whole realm of nature, a unique action of the total universe. This reality is rarely, if ever, experienced by most individuals. Even those who know it to be true in theory do not sense or feel it, but continue to believe themselves to be isolated 'egos' inside bags of skin."

We don't experience ourselves as an expression of the whole universe because we are listening to a conversation that creates the illusion of separation. Every interaction is evidence that you are different, other. You don't belong here, in this group, in this situation.
**The real message is
you don't belong in life.**

Separating us from the herd is achieved through a number of conversations:

-- a conversation that sets up "me versus them."

They don't like me.
They hate me.
I can't be who I am and be accepted.
I'm different from them. I don't fit in.
They're laughing at me.
They think I'm stupid.
I'm not welcome. I'm always an outsider.
They're just being polite. They don't really want me here.
It's them. They're judgmental. I don't really want to be with them anyway.
They're all out to get me. If I put myself out there, they **will** get me.

-- a conversation in which the universe is unfriendly, creating a sense of "me versus life."

The world is unsafe.
It's all so unpredictable.
You never know what's going to happen
Things are out of control.

People are dangerous, mean, unpredictable and insensitive.

Life is so unfair.

No one cares about me. I'm in this all by myself.

No one understands you. You're all alone.

-- a conversation of general messages suggesting that "I" am left out because there is something wrong with "me."

I will never be successful; I don't have what it takes.

You don't fit in, you never have. Wrong family, wrong schools, wrong you.

If you had something to contribute, perhaps they would invite you to the group.

Everyone else fits in. I feel so left out.

You can't say what you feel.

You hurt people every time you open your mouth.

I will never have a meaningful relationship.

You don't know how to behave, so you can't be around others.

Nobody likes you.

You are so inarticulate.

You are toxic; you're dangerous to others.

No one loves me. No one even sees me.

I'm not lovable or attractive.

You're too tired to make the effort to go out.
No one wants you there anyway.
Nobody cares how you feel.
You can't afford to do that.

The hunter (the con artist) makes sure its isolated prey doesn't rejoin the pack. It whispers its "good advice," ensuring I don't do anything to reach out, connect, participate, or engage in life. I must be kept away from all proof that I-don't-belong is completely made up, that the whole thing is just a story.

The best thing for you is to just stay home.
Don't go out. Don't engage any more than you have to.
Don't say anything. Better to keep silent and be thought a fool than open your mouth and prove it.
This is your problem; keep it to yourself.
If you shut up at least you don't have to endure the humiliation of pity.
Better to reject than be rejected.
Better to stay a little disappointed than to risk big disappointment.
Better to hole up, hunker down, know your limits so you can stay within them.

Don't try. Don't risk. If you don't try you won't fail.
Keep your head down; if they can't see you, they can't get you.

But if the story of isolation is threatened, if there is an invitation to experience belonging, we are conned into defending our prison, parroting back the excuses we have been fed, arguing for our story as "my truth," the one thing that cannot be taken from me.

I'm probably better off staying at home.
They don't really want me.
I don't really belong there.

In this way the ego system enslaves us, causing us to feel excluded and defensive. Resentment of the group vies with longing for connection, the "safety" of the status quo versus the desire to break out. The voices talk us into behaving in ways that push people away, furthering our sense of isolation. Yes, we are required to relate and interact in daily life, but the "other" remains the enemy. Herein lies the heart of the bamboozle. The only relationship we are left with, our one constant companion, is a hateful, manipulative voice in the head that has brainwashed us into giving our life force to it. We can't see that our "reality of separation" is a complete illusion.

This is the quintessential abusive relationship in which cruelty has come to be perceived as love, support, truth, and reality.

This bamboozle is one of the reasons the Buddha left us with the Three Jewels: Bodhi (truth, enlightenment, awakening), Dharma (cosmic law/order/teachings), and Sangha (community of those who practice together). Sangha is our best protection against the predatory con artist, keeping us from becoming isolated prey. We walk together with a community because if we don't it's pretty much guaranteed that we walk with the con artist.

Practicing together allows us to see the stories we hear in conditioned mind, the stories we are fed, are not personal, that the whole process is universal. Everyone hears essentially the same information. You're bad, you can't be trusted, you're selfish, a phony, a liar.... Everyone believes what's being done to them is their fault. Everyone projects their lot is worse than everyone else's and the reason is there is something wrong with them.

When we see other people—good, sincere people—living out the same stories that have enslaved us, we can finally see the stories as lies. Seeing the universality of how suffering is caused by the lies replaces isolation with compassion for all. When we come together, the illusion of separation is replaced by connection, intimacy, safety, compassion, understanding, support, and kindness.

The way out of this particular bamboozle is to cultivate a strong relationship with the Mentor. As soon as we get into relationship with "someone" who knows our goodness, a supportive rather than abusive relationship, we're on the path to freedom. Our work, our practice, is to accept that goodness is our True Nature, that we **are** expressions of the Intelligence That Animates ALL, and to take that walk to freedom.

Illusion of Separation Assignment: Week One

As you go about your day, catch the con artist conjuring the **illusion** of separation.

Listen for the conversations that create a sense of "me versus them."

Example: I don't fit into that group. They don't like me.

Hear the conversations that create a sense of "me versus life."

Example: "Life is so unfair."

 At the end of each day, record your insights and awarenesses about how the illusion of a "me" separate from Life is created and maintained.

Illusion of Separation Assignment: Week Two

When we are HERE, present, in the moment, we don't experience a sense of feeling isolated or separate.

This week support yourself in having the experience of connection that comes from not listening to the voices in conditioned mind. Each time you recognize a conversation of "separation," pick up your recorder and talk about what you appreciate in your life, what you are grateful for, what is beautiful around you, what you love. Listen to the recording and let yourself have the experience that **presence is connection.**

At the end of each day, listen to the day's recordings.

Illusion of Separation Assignment: Week Three

The con artist often creates separation by spinning a story that I am not acceptable because there is something wrong with me.

To counter this, write the love letter you've always wanted to receive. Write as many letters as required to "get it right." When you're satisfied with it **for now**—you can keep writing, recording, and listening to these for the rest of your life—record it and listen to it. Pay close attention to what it feels like to **receive** what is said in the letter.

**When attention is on love,
there is no illusion of separation.**

Note: The con artist is going to work hard to sabotage this exercise. Listen for what the voices say to 1) stop you from writing the letter, 2) stop you from recording and listening to it, and 3) stop you from believing what the letter contains.

A voice that says "I don't like the sound of my voice" or "that sounds phony" or "you don't sound sincere" is ALWAYS the con artist!

Illusion of Separation Assignment: Week Four

The conversation is often about how "I" don't belong or they don't like me. In persuading us to identify with the "victim," the con artist can keep us isolated and feeling alone.

The truth is that we are each part of All That Is. When we come from a conviction of belonging, we feel open, helpful, kind, and caring. This week, practice connection by saying something kind to, or doing something kind for, the people with whom you interact.

Record your experience of non-separation as attention is on connection!

 At the end of each day, listen to your recordings from the day.

BAMBOOZLE NO. 10

A man traveling across a field encountered a tiger. He fled, the tiger after him.

Coming to a precipice, he caught hold of the root of a wild vine and swung himself down over the edge. The tiger sniffed at him from above. Trembling, the man looked down to where, far below, another tiger was waiting to eat him. Only the vine sustained him.

Two mice, one white and one black, little by little started to gnaw away at the vine. The man saw a luscious strawberry near him. Grasping the vine with one hand, he plucked the strawberry with the other. How sweet it tasted!
--*Zen Flesh, Zen Bones*

This old Zen story is a powerful reminder to live in the moment. However precarious our circumstances, there is a sweetness in Life that is the product of being HERE for it. To be alive is a gift that can be enjoyed only if we acknowledge that Life is transience and this moment is all we have.

The Buddha taught Life is flux, all formations are transient. If we pay attention, our experience of life is a deep awareness of this truth. Stars burn and collapse, civilizations rise and fall, species evolve and go extinct, we grow old and die. And yet this truth rarely touches how we live our lives. A false sense of continuity lulls us into postponing living NOW for a vague belief that there will be time to live "later."

For example:
I don't have time to begin a meditation practice now.
I'll call mom tomorrow.
I bet I can squeeze that workout in this afternoon instead.
There's too much to do. Perhaps I can take that vacation next month.

Introducing Ego Bamboozle No. 10: PERMANENCE

We suffer deeply when the illusion of permanence

is shattered by reality—the death of a loved one, the breakup of a cherished relationship, the loss of a job, a life-threatening illness. Our surprise when things change reveals the extent to which we assume life will stay the same.

The con artist does not want us to notice all that arises passes away. What better way to keep attention engaged in perpetual dissatisfaction than to have it chasing, grasping, craving, desiring, and longing for permanence in a transient world? As Thich Nhat Hanh says, "We suffer not because things are impermanent, but because we believe they should not be."

Just as rapidly moving pictures in a film create the illusion of continuous action, the con artist creates sequence, sense, continuity, causality, and meaning by interpreting what arises in the moment. Caught in that illusion of permanence, we are out of sync with the pulse of Life, and the dissonance registers as dissatisfaction. The sensations of discord are folded into a story of anxiety, insecurity, and something wrong with life. It's simple misdirection, intended to distract us from recognizing that "what's wrong" is a result of attending to a conversation instead of **directly** experiencing Life. The conversation is always one beat behind what is HERE, always out of step with Life.

Being conned out of living in the NOW creates some familiar problems:

Procrastination
We are familiar with the adage, "There is no time like the present." There isn't! And yet we mightily resist doing what needs to be done in the moment. A voice says, "I don't have time now. There'll be time to do it later. I need to attend to this first." We postpone, we reschedule, we procrastinate. The moment passes.

-- We don't pay a bill and our credit lapses.
-- We neglect to cancel an appointment and are charged a fee.
-- We don't address an issue with a colleague, and it's blown out of proportion.

Eventually, we come to and feel angry, discouraged, helpless or disappointed that once again we failed to be "on top of it." It's a perfect set-up. We're talked into a belief that there is a "later," and then beaten up for believing there is. We're left to face the consequences of our behaviors, and the con artist gets a big, juicy meal from our suffering.

Even worse, we're programmed to believe we can have later what we don't practice now. For example, I live in a conversation that makes me anxious because there is "so much to do and so little time to do it." I get talked into postponing relaxation, fun, and rest as the voice assures me there will be time later. But when later becomes now, I find I don't know how to relax or have fun. Not because relaxation is not possible if I just dropped into Life's rhythm, **but because I have not learned how to drop out of the conversation that makes me anxious!**

Urgency
"I'm late! I'm late for a very important date! No time to say `Hello,' `Goodbye,' I'm late, I'm late, I'm late!"
Alice's Adventures in Wonderland by Lewis Carroll

We can all relate to the White Rabbit running out of time and being in a stew. **If procrastination is the sense of "plenty of time to take care of things** later," urgency is "not enough time to get it done now."

Urgency is yet another story in conditioned mind, perpetuating the illusion of permanence. It is the direct result of attending to a conversation rather than being in tune with Life's rhythm.

We're talked into believing we have an elastic capacity to do things, tricked into setting unreasonable deadlines, assuming we can manipulate time to get it all done. "Oh, sure, I can do that, and that, and that." We miscalculate what can be accomplished in the time available. "Oh, sure, that should take about an hour, which will leave me plenty of time to...." The to-do list grows, as do urgency and overwhelm. The voices stoke the urgency, whispering "time's running out, not enough time, too much to do."

Always running, trying to keep up, anxiety dogs us wherever we go. We skip meals, sleep less, drop the gym class—prioritizing urgency over what takes care of us. Eventually, we run out of steam and crash. We don't get it all done, or we do it poorly, and are once again bamboozled into accepting that "it's my fault."

Time Management

The con artist's solution for the devastation wreaked by urgency and procrastination is "time management." It convinces us our problem is inefficiency, and that we need forecasting, budgeting, and scheduling skills to grab control and avoid "wasting" time. We can learn how not to waste time, how to make or find enough time, how to ensure we don't run out of time, even how to manage to be just in time.

The belief that we can control time causes frustration more often than it delivers the promised efficiency of time management classes.

We are
-- impatient if we have to wait for things to happen.
-- disappointed if things don't happen when we expect them to.
-- frustrated that we can't make things happen on our schedule.

And, yet, when we stop to take a breath, when we drop into the moment, we experience Life unfolding at a sustainable pace. Life grows babies and blooms flowers and pays bills with relaxed ease.

In Taoism this principle is referred to as *wu wei*, doing/non-doing, or effortless action.

Conditioned mind often frames this effortless action as passive—but it is anything but passive. When we turn attention away from the conversation about Life in conditioned mind, we drop into the process of Intelligence in action, expressing itself in perfect dynamic movement through form. In the words of Stephen Mitchell, the "doer vanishes into the deed." We cannot tell "the dancer from the dance." We experience "the Tao never does anything, yet through it all things are done."

At this point, the con artist jumps in and argues "You'll never get anything done with that attitude." But that's just more of the conversation in conditioned mind we have to get out of! We must let go the conditioned conversation and discover the energy and action of HERE, NOW.

Buddhism is often described as the negative way and framed as a philosophy of abstinence and denial—framed that way by egocentric karmic conditioning/self-hate, of course. The focus on death and transience is called "morbid" by the ego and, we're advised, is best avoided. But that is, as we say in Zen, hogwash! The Buddha's teaching to accept the transience of life is encouragement to be joyfully present, to delight in the moment, to recognize and embrace our Authentic Nature as Life unfolding.

As Alan Watts says, "You may believe yourself out of harmony with life and its eternal Now, but you cannot be, for you are life and exist in Now — otherwise you would not be here."

We are always in the NOW. We cannot not be. Direct experience of that is a matter of learning to turn attention to NOW rather than being bamboozled by a conversation about an illusory reality where time is under our control. When we're HERE, fully present, we experience Life with vivid intensity.

Katagiri Roshi encourages, "You have to do your best to face every moment, because this moment will never come again. The moment that you are living right now is a very important opportunity to make your life vividly alive. If you want to live with spiritual security in the midst of constant change, you have to burn the flame of your life force in everything you do."

Permanence Assignment: Week One

This week spend some time with this question:
What do you assume there will be time to do in the future?

Example:
I can always talk to my father later.
I'll meditate this evening instead of this morning.

A fun way to do this assignment: Put up a large white sheet of paper on a wall. When something that you assume you can do later occurs to you, write it on the paper.

At the end of each day, record how grateful and blessed you are to have had, and to be having, this day!

At the end of the week, review the things you didn't do because you were told you could do them later. See how the con artist robs you by talking you into not living in thisherenow.

Do it later!

Permanence Assignment: Week Two

This week, catch the trickster in the process of persuading you to procrastinate. When you hear a conversation about postponing something, practice attending to it NOW. Pay attention as the voices debate, argue, cajole, resist, forget, and negotiate to **not** do X in the moment. Do it NOW.

Make a recording at the beginning of the week to remind you that you are practicing attending to Now instead of indulging procrastination. Listen to it each morning

At the end of each day, make a celebration recording of all the things you attended to and how good it feels to have taken care of what the scam attempted to get you to postpone.

Permanence Assignment: Week Three

This week, pay attention to how you are conned into being urgent, in a rush, harried. Like a reporter following a story, watch how urgency unfolds. What do the voices say to make you feel you are out of time? What behaviors do they talk you into that result in the belief that you need to be urgent? Do you take on too much? Are you not able to keep track of how much time you have? Are you talked into distractions that steal your time?

When you feel the sensations of urgency, stop, take a couple of nice, long, deep breaths, and relax into thisherenow. Record what you see about how listening to the story of not-enough-time/urgency is a distraction from being focused and efficient with the task at hand.

At the end of each day, make a recording that assists you to relax into thisherenow. Listen to this recording the next day each time the con artist starts a conversation of urgency.

Permanence Assignment: Week Four

This week's assignment is to pay attention to impermanence. Set a timer during the day. When the timer goes off, take a couple of moments to record some of the things around you that are moving, changing, coming into and going out of existence. Allow yourself to be in tune with the constant flux of life.

Example: Clouds pass by, breezes move through trees, birds dart from branch to branch, breath rises and falls....

 At the end of the day, record your insights and observations about being part of and in tune with the changing energies of life.

BAMBOOZLE NO. 11

"The Miracle of Living"

Bankei was a famous Zen teacher. His lectures were tremendously popular. People traveled far and wide to hear what he had to say.

On one occasion, Bankei happened to be teaching next to a local Buddhist school. The students of this school, excited by the opportunity to learn from a "true Master," decided to skip school and attend Bankei's talk.

The local teacher arrived to find his classroom empty.

Envious of Bankei's popularity, the teacher decided to challenge Bankei to a debate. Arriving at the square where Bankei was holding forth, the teacher started to harangue his students to create a commotion and disrupt the proceedings. Bankei was forced to stop his lecture and face the challenger.

The local teacher boasted that his lineage was more exalted than Bankei's.

"My teacher," he said, "could stand on one bank of the river, recite the sutras, and make them appear on a parchment I was holding on the other side of the river. Can you perform such miracles?"

Bankei shook his head and replied lightly.

"The only miracle I perform," he said, "is to eat when I am hungry, and sleep when I am tired!" -- Adapted from an old Zen Story.

Really? To eat when hungry and sleep when tired is hardly the stuff of miracles, is it? Eating and sleeping are **just life**, ordinary routines, like washing dishes and brushing teeth. A miracle is a bigger, better, unexpected, otherworldly, highly improbable, and extraordinary event that cannot be explained rationally! Isn't it?

If we dismissed Bankei's miracle as "nothing extraordinary," then we have just experienced Ego Bamboozle No. 11: CONTENT VS. PROCESS. Because, in fact, being alive **is** a miracle and Life **is** miraculous.

If we pause even for a moment to be present to the rustle of the wind in the leaves, the dance of the hummingbird, the brilliant moon peeping out behind the clouds, the joyous ebullience of a cherry tree in full bloom, the graceful descent of a waterfall, the melting brown eyes of a puppy, or the tiny, perfect fingers of a baby, we experience joy that breaks the heart open. The wonder of existence pervades our being.

"There are only two ways to live your life. One is as though nothing is a miracle. The other is as though everything is a miracle." -- Albert Einstein

It seems only children live in the high-energy of curiosity, play, and wonder in which everything is fascinating. The rest of us are so focused on the mundane day-to-day that marveling at the miracle of Life is lost. We accept as a matter of course that being a responsible adult means leaving behind carefree childhood for the serious business of getting through the day.

Over time, living becomes an endless series of "whats," the **stuff** (working, errands, traffic, kids, parents, meetings) that fills our days. Ceaseless **doing** drains enthusiasm, vitality, and our sense of being alive. Feeling depleted, we turn to our pick-me-up of choice—caffeine, sugar, alcohol, sex, drugs, extreme sports—or to novelty—new job, new relationship, new car—anything to experience excitement of some kind. If the current "what" is no longer that interesting, a new "what" must be found!

We embark with eagerness and anticipation on our new interest—building a deck, writing a book, remodeling the kitchen. It's fun for a while, but inevitably the excitement fades. Some aspect of the project proves to be too challenging, frustrating, or boring, the "high" wears off, and the "grind" is back. We lose interest, shelve the project, and add it to our list of "what in the world was I thinking" or "chalk up another failure." No matter how often this pattern repeats, we fall for the lure of novelty, the seduction of "new," with the same results. It doesn't occur to us to question whether the issue is not with "what I do" but rather with "how I do it."

The difference between our childhood and adult experience of life is not that Life is less joyful or miraculous as we age; it is that we have been conned into believing joy is a **result** of **what** we do.

The Buddha taught Life is flux, an ever-changing, dynamic, coming together and falling apart. Life is a **how**, not a what; it is **process**, not content. Everything is changing all the time. Yes, Life is full of stuff, innumerable whats, but if we pay attention, we notice that the content of Life is perceived as static only because we have a conditioned and erroneous way of seeing it.

Everyone recognizes this drawing as a tree. We "know" it's a tree. But the word "tree" and this drawing do not capture the living, breathing marvel of Life that is a tree. Standing before a tree, we can sense Life unfolding in the colors of the leaves, the texture of the bark, the fragrance of the flowers, the movement of the branches, the complex processes of food production, respiration, transpiration, reproduction, decay, and growth contained in its towering presence. Reducing the tree to an object, to a "what," renders us incapable of appreciating it for the miracle it is.

It's not the **job** that is exciting or the **relationship** that is fulfilling or the **vacation** that is relaxing or the **idea** that is inspiring or the **gathering** that is joyful. Excitement, fulfillment, relaxation, inspiration, and joy may be nouns in our language but they are **verbs** in Life. They are "processes," independent of the content, or object, to which they have been associated.

The con artist bamboozles us into believing that it's the "stuff" that's important, and we cease to be present to how we are with the stuff.

Content is static, abstract, dead; the juice is in the process of living. But because the CONversation in CONditioned mind focuses our attention on the CONtent, we miss being **present and participatiing in the process.**

No wonder we feel drained and depleted after we fall for this bamboozle and throw all of our energy into acquiring the next object that promises "excitement."

Content disappoints; presence fulfills.

In giving attention to the "what," we stop attending to the "how" and the energy of existence is siphoned off to feed ego's survival system.

With Awareness Practice, we discover that when we stop attending to the conversation in conditioned mind, we stop fueling what fossilizes our lives. Instead of feeding a process that keeps the sense of "ego-I" alive, we can enjoy the process of being animated by Life. In participating in the "how" of existence, we tap into the energy of being alive. We feel "lively." It's not **what** we do, but **how** we do it that becomes the focus of attention. We can experience joy, enthusiasm, inspiration, curiosity, love, and kindness with anything we are present to. Engaging in process, gives us an **alive** experience of **living!**

-- When we care for something, we feel cared for.
-- When we express love for something, we feel loved.

-- When we are curious about life, we experience a sense of adventure.
-- When we are wholly present, we feel part of all that is.

In the dynamic unfolding of the Intelligence That Animates, we realize every moment is new. This moment will never be again. Instead of seeking novelty, we can be present to the miracle of THIS, HERE, NOW. **Whatever** we do is embraced in the freshness, the beauty, and the wonder of Life unfolding.

Enlightenment is being HERE for the life we have, present and participating. This is why the highest form of Zen is the "fool." The enlightenment of this jolly, happy being, dancing with children in the marketplace, comes from real-izing the extraordinariness of ordinary life. Eating when hungry and sleeping when tired are true miracles of being alive.

Content vs. Process Assignment: Week One

The practice this week is to look for the ordinary miracles in your life and to catalog them. Put up a large white sheet of paper on a wall. Write or draw all the miracles you notice.

Examples:
Fresh water flows from the tap when I turn it on.
I can spring out of bed in the morning!
Add your own....

 Make recordings at the end of the day that document the miracles in the ordinary.

Content vs. Process Assignment: Week Two

The con artist keeps talking us out of what takes care of us. We don't get to eat when we're hungry or sleep when we're tired. Instead we're tricked into behaviors that cause us to go unconscious about healthy choices.

This week practice Bankei's miracle. Eat (healthy food) when you are hungry and sleep when you are tired.

At the beginning of the week, make a recording prioritizing nutrition and sleep. Listen to it each morning and evening.

Pay attention to the various ways the con artist endeavors to interfere with your plans.

Content vs. Process Assignment: Week Three

Practice the "miracle of a tree." Choose something beautiful and alive whose existence has been pushed to the periphery of your awareness.

Set aside 15 minutes a day to be present and engaged in this "what" (content) as a "how" (process). Notice how giving full attention changes your experience of a "what." Record and Listen to your insights.

At the end of each day, listen to your recordings.

Content vs. Process Assignment: Week Four

This week cultivate a process approach. Decide on a process such as loving, caring, or giving. Bring attention to the **process** with whatever you do.

-- Prepare a meal lovingly
-- Care for the plant, the dog, and the kids enthusiastically.
-- Give yourself completely to the drive to work, the yoga class, the meeting....

Watch how the voices attempt to talk you out of experiencing the process you have chosen to attend to. Persist in attending despite all conversations about your efforts not working.

Listening to a voice saying "it's not working" is practicing a process of not working!

At the end of each day, record and listen to what it feels like to participate in the process of Life instead of the content of conditioned mind.

BAMBOOZLE NO. 12

"Who are you?" said the Caterpillar.

This was not an encouraging opening for a conversation. Alice replied, rather shyly, "I— I hardly know, Sir, at present—at least I know who I was when I got up this morning, but I think I must have changed several times since then."

"What do you mean by that?" said the Caterpillar, sternly. "Explain yourself!"

"I can't explain myself, I'm afraid, Sir," said Alice, "because I'm not myself, you see."
-- *Alice's Adventures in Wonderland* by Lewis Carroll

Almost every spiritual quest begins with the caterpillar's question. The sense in which we ask the question is a wondering about life, the universe, and our place in it. If we continue to explore this line of inquiry, our answer might be closer to Alice's than we think and will reveal a "bamboozle" that is earthshaking in its implications.

If we don't stop to examine it, we might respond to the Caterpillar's question of "Who are you?" with a name, a label, a description that points to a person, a "someone," an "I," who is the sum of all the attributes, history, experiences, memories, foibles, eccentricities... that capture "me," the person I believe myself to be. But what if who "I" believe "I" am is not what "I" really am?

Introducing Ego Bamboozle No. 12: I-LLUSION

Almost every con game relies on the ability of the perpetrator to convince their mark of the existence of something that doesn't exist— imaginary gold mines, fictional sweepstakes, illusory investment opportunities, the ultimate dream business/romantic partner, non-existent inheritances, etc. So long as the mark believes in the illusion, the con is in play.

If we pay attention to the voices of egocentric karmic conditioning/self-hate, we notice that the central purpose of the conversation is keeping a sense of "self" alive, ensuring that "I" is the focus of attention.

Here are some examples.

Self-Pity: Woe is me! No one loves me. I might as well not exist. I can't say what I want. I can never get what I want. Life is too difficult.

Self-Hate: I'm so stupid! I can't do anything right. I'm such a failure.

Self-destruction: I'm on a diet but I'm going to eat that last piece of cake. I know I have to get up early tomorrow, but I'm going to stay up and watch that movie. I know it's not good for me, but just this once...

Self-Improvement: I have to fix me. I am going to lose 5 pounds, get a trainer, stay away from Facebook, and meditate more. If I do all these things, I am going to be happy, have a better life, be loved and accepted.

Self-Preservation: I need to fight for my rights. He needs to be told he cannot push me around! She needs to be knocked down a peg! I don't want to do what she tells me to do. You are wrong. I don't feel like it. Not listening to you. I know what's good for me.

Self-Indulgence: I deserve this. I want more— more time, more money, more attention, more space, more cake....

Self-Consciousness: I can't say anything so I won't say anything. What must they think of me! I'm so embarrassed.

Self-Absorbed: Why are you so upset that I haven't written? I don't really care what you want to do. This is what I want to do! It's a drought but I can water my lawns any time I want. I don't need to use headphones while I run in the park. Who cares if it interferes with someone else's wish for quiet?

Self-Defense: I was provoked; he deserved it. It was her fault; she shouldn't have said that.

Self-Assertion: I need to take control of the situation. Let me tell you how it's going to go. I will prove to you I'm right.

Self-sacrifice: I will eat lunch at my desk so I can keep working on this presentation. I don't have the time but I will take on that extra credit assignment. I'll go to the store even though I'm exhausted.

Self-doubt: My hair looks awful! Did I forget to close the garage door? Will I enjoy myself at the party? Am I okay? Does she like me? Did I do well in that presentation? Did they approve of what I said? I wonder if what I'm wearing is appropriate. Is this the right job for me? I am so different from him.

Self-Centered: What do I like? Who do I dislike? What do I want for dinner? What am I afraid of? What am I doing tomorrow? Where am I going? When will I get through my check-list? I have too much to do!

Reading the above examples, we might conclude that this is just "me" talking. But if we allow ourselves to stop and really pay attention, we might see that the **conversation** is what conjures the "I" into existence. Without the conversation, there is no sense of "me" and Alice's response to the Caterpillar starts to make sense!

Interestingly, the "I" in these conversations is needy, neurotic, phobic, inadequate, worried, grasping, depressed, overworked, over-anxious, tentative, scared, fixated, and obsessed. This is a suffering "someone," convinced there is something wrong with them or with their lives, spending the vast majority of their time focused on themselves. Why do we do this?

This quote from *Ask the Awakened* by Wei Wu Wei offers a clue: "Why do you suffer? Because 99.9% of everything you think, and of everything you do, is for yourself—and there isn't one."

Since suffering produces the energy for the ego-identity system to survive, what better way to keep the con game going in perpetuity than to convince a human being that they **are** the ego-identity? I'm flawed and my lifelong pursuit must be to create, maintain, define, improve, shape, and defend an identity that does not exist.

The biggest consequence of falling for this particular bamboozle is we ignore what we authentically are. We "forget" we are unique expressions of the Intelligence That Animates; we "forget" we are built to receive and transmit the energies of Life. And we "forget" we can experience the full spectrum of consciousness. We are talked out of **realizing** we have the capacity to **express Life**—all movements, moods, energies and sensations.

Like a negative in photography, the ego experience is always a story of what's not.

For example: If my life has been blessed by abundance, well-being, and prosperity, the conversation is about scarcity, lack, and deprivation. When I'm in the story, my experience is absence of abundance, not enjoyment of it.

Because I am a genuinely kind, friendly, and compassionate human, the con artist feeds me stories of all the hateful and unkind things I have, supposedly, said and done. It points out how hateful and unkind everyone is. The universe becomes a hostile place in which I feel alone and isolated.

Identified with ego, we experience a stripped, limited, narrow version of "reality." **Believing we are the illusory "I," we have an ego experience of existence, not a Life experience.** When the lens of ego defines our perspective, we stop being able to see Life as it is.

In this way, we lose our ability to move with the flow of the river of Life, to navigate its rapids, to explore its depths, to luxuriate in the shallows, and to thoroughly enjoy the ride. **We are reduced to conditioned reactions to Life arising.**

To follow up on our previous examples:

I have plenty of money but I hesitate to give a generous tip at the restaurant, even though the service has been superb and the waiter really friendly. The conditioned reaction to friendliness and service is a lack of generosity and appreciation because the I-llusion is only focused on loss and hostility!

A survival focus

The struggle for survival is based on fear, on the belief there is not enough and we must vigilantly defend against a dangerous world. This stance fuels competition, aggression, and anxiety. This might sound dramatic, but here are some examples in our daily lives.

"He complimented her, not me."
"I got here first! Get in line"
"It's him or me. He has to go. I can't deal with him."

Since the ego-I is only interested in its own survival, and since its world-view is scarcity, exclusion, and fear, when we identify with "ego-I" we act in unfortunate ways.

On a macro level, a survival focus dictates the prevailing attitude towards the stewardship of the planet, the use of resources, the wars that are fought, or the "rights" that are defended. "All for one and one for all" is not ego-I's motto!

On a more "personal" level, we find ourselves saying hateful things, doing things we're horrified we did when we come to, behaving in ways we genuinely regret, and acting in ways people who know us say is uncharacteristic. Then we rationalize with "That wasn't like me, I wasn't myself, I must have been out of my mind," or some equivalent.

Awareness Practice trains us to see the con game as a conversation in the head that captures the attention. We learn tools to direct attention away from that conversation, thereby grounding us in the present. In the present, we experience life as it is. We discover the universe is friendly, and it is possible to collaborate, connect, coexist, and flourish beyond the ego's struggle to survive. We develop an experience of being more than the limited "I" defined by the "conversation."

Disidentifying from the illusory "I" is the hardest thing we do.

We are conditioned to take everything personally. Ego is the process of taking what is universal and impersonal and making it about "me." Reversing that process requires us to give up the notion that "I" am at the center of the universe, a position that "I" has jealously guarded!

If all the attention is not on an illusory "me," it is possible to see what else is here. Instead of our life force being in service to an ego survival system, we have a chance to be truly helpful and of service to what Life calls us to be. "Live a joyful, grateful life!" is another way of saying "being in service to what Life is calling us to."

I-llusion Assignment: Week One

The conversation in conditioned mind creates an illusory sense of a "me," a "self" separate from the rest of life.

This week catch the con artist creating this illusion by paying attention to any conversation in conditioned mind that comes under the categories of self-defense, self-hate, self-pity, self-destruction, self-preservation, self-assertion.... For examples of these, re-read the text of the bamboozle.

At the end of each day, record your insights and awarenesses of the extent to which the conversation defines "me" and limits authentic expression.

For extra credit, make a recording of what might be expressed authentically in the absence of a conversation that limits and defines "me."

Example: "You are not artistic" is the message I hear. Without that conversation, I can sign up for a watercolor class and have fun creating.

I-llusion Assignment: Week Two

This week the focus is on developing a picture of "who I am." As you go about your day, jot down any voices you hear that describe "you," that answer the question "I am the sort of person who...." You can use a journal or notepad for this exercise.

Examples:
I like ice cream.
I don't go to bed on time.
You hate it if someone tells you what to do.

Spend some time questioning if this information is fact or propaganda. Is this always true? Record your insights about expanding your sense of who you are beyond ego's definitions.

I-llusion Assignment: Week Three

What if the "me" is not all you are? This week challenge the identities that you have accepted as "me." For example:

Read about something that "I" is not interested in.
Taste a dish that "I" doesn't like.
Do something "I" doesn't want to do (a dance class, a massage).
Don't defend an idea that "I" clings to.
Pursue something "I" wants to avoid.
Listen to music that "I" doesn't like.
Be open to exploring something that "I" resists.

What do the voices say when the identity is challenged?

At the end of each day, record and listen to what it's like not to be just a "me."

Note: Don't let the con artist talk you into something that does not take care of you!

I-llusion Assignment: Week Four

"Taking it personally" is one of the ways the con artist ensures that the illusion of an "I" is maintained.

Example: I get upset when my boss ignores my suggestions.

What would life be like if you were not identifying with the "I" that takes things personally? Find out this week.

At the end of each day, record and listen to your experience of life when "everything is not about me!"

CONclusion

We've just explored twelve of the most common ways egocentric karmic conditioning/self-hate bamboozles us. Are there more? Absolutely!

It can seem that the bamboozles are infinite, but that's just another bamboozle! The con artist will use any and everything to capture our attention because, while content is infinite, the process is definitely finite.

The swindle that bilks a person out of five dollars can be used on a hundred, a thousand, a million dollars, a house, a car or a boat. The object may change but the deception remains the same.

What all bamboozles have in common is that they grab our attention and drag us out of thisherenow into a phony, imaginary, faux reality of something wrong and not enough maintained through a conversation in conditioned mind.

Therefore, there is only one way to put the con artist out of business and end suffering-----

STOP giving attention to the conversation.
It is that simple.

There is nothing to understand, nothing to figure out, and nothing to learn by listening to what the voices say. Any relationship with conditioned mind gives life force to maintaining the con game.

End the Conversation. End the Con Game.
That is the end game.

One additional bamboozle to watch for:
You are practicing along, but the con artist keeps tripping you up. You keep falling for the same bamboozles over and over. Soon you will hear "This isn't working. You can't do this. Just quit."

If you don't quit, don't be surprised if you hear "You should just kill yourself." When you hear you should quit or you should kill yourself, you can know you are winning the game. The con artist is on the run and desperate.

Keep going.
Pick up the pace.
And end the conversation about how you are doing!

Afterword

People will ask:

"Why do we suffer?"
"Why does egocentric karmic conditioning/self-hate exist?"
"Why do we even have an ego?"

These questions are similar to:

"Where do we go when we die?
"Is there a God?"

The Buddha refused to entertain these questions for the simple reason that nobody knows. He taught that being fully present will give us all the information we need.

When we are fully present, "that which questions" is absent!

These simple lines from Zen poet Ryokan express the experience of the movement to pure presence.

"Like the little stream
making its way
through the mossy crevices,
I, too, quietly
turn clear and transparent."

There is one why question that is perhaps worth
considering.

Why should we practice awareness?

The Buddha has a marvelous answer to that
question as well.

His answer: There is no reason to.

It's a choice.

It's a choice we exercise when we become aware
there must be more to life than the dissatisfaction
we feel when our life force is in service to an ego
maintenance system.

When we choose to cultivate a practice of
awareness, we develop access to a way of being
that is profoundly joyful. The "normal" lens
through which the world is viewed, with its divisions

and boundaries of "self and other," is transformed. We open to what all religious and spiritual traditions refer to as the mystical and indescribable "one-ness with all that is." In this transformation, we discover we are authentic expressions of love, compassion, kindness, understanding, and wisdom.

In the words of Nisargadutta Maharaj: "When you know beyond all doubting that the same life flows through all that is and you are that life, you will love all naturally and spontaneously. When you realize the depth and fullness of yourself, you know that every living being and the entire universe are included in your affection. But when you look at anything as separate from you, you cannot love it for you are afraid of it. Alienation causes fear and fear deepens alienation."

We might still wonder why we have to feel separate, afraid, and dissatisfied. Why does it require a journey of transformation before we rest in the joyful discovery of our True Nature as love and compassion?

If we stay with wondering why, that's what we're likely to have: a life of wondering why.

"Philosophy is speculation. Zen is participation."
-- Bhagwan Shree Rajneesh.

We need to walk the path, to be open to "what else," to a different "how," if we choose to have a life other than that of the voices of egocentric karmic conditioning/self-hate.

Is it worth it? We get to find out for ourselves!

It does require us to want to!

"Now is now. Are you going to be here or not?"
-- Ram Dass

))

TALK WITH CHERI

Open Air
Talk Radio
Open Air is Cheri's internet-based call-in radio show.
Call in, listen, and download archived shows at
www.livingcompassion.org.

Online Classes
Cheri conducts interactive online classes via e-mail
on a wide variety of subjects
related to Zen Awareness Practice.
To be notified of future classes
sign up at www.livingcompassion.org.

Cheri's Practice Blog
Follow "Cheri Huber's Practice Blog"
at http://cherispracticeblog.blogspot.com

Books and Recordings
All Cheri Huber titles are available from your local
independent bookstore or online at www.keepitsimple.org.
Also available online are audio downloads and DVDs.

Visit www.livingcompassion.org to:

Sign up to receive notice of new email classes with Cheri Huber

Find a schedule of workshops and retreats

Find meditation groups in your area

Sign up for Reflective Listening Buddies

Sign up for Practice Everywhere

Sign up for a Zen Awareness Coach

Sign up for a Recording and Listening Trainer

Find out about our work in an impoverished community
in Zambia. Read blogs with updates from
the Africa Vulnerable Children Project.

Email: information@livingcompassion.org
Telephone: 209-728-0860

Visit www.recordingandlistening.org
Read articles, access resources, challenge yourself
to fun exercises and get inspired!
You can even share your favorite
Recording and Listening insights and practices.

There Is Nothing Wrong With You

An Extraordinary Eight-Day Retreat
based on the book
There Is Nothing Wrong With You: Going Beyond Self-Hate
by Cheri Huber

Inside each of us is a "persistent voice of discontent." It is constantly critical of life, the world, and almost everything we say and do. As children, in order to survive, we learned to listen to this voice and believe what it says.

This retreat is eight days of looking directly at how we are rejected and punished by the voices of self-hate and discovering how to let that go. Through a variety of exercises and periods of group processing, participants gain a clearer perspective on how they live their lives and on how to find compassion for themselves and others.

This work is challenging, joyous, fulfilling, scary, courageous, demanding, freeing, loving, kind, and compassionate—compassionate toward yourself and everyone you will ever know.

For information on attending, contact:
Living Compassion/Zen Monastery Peace Center
P.O. Box 1756
Murphys, CA 95247
Ph.: 209-728-0860
Email: information@livingcompassion.org
Website: www.livingcompassion.org

What You Practice Is What You Have is a sequel to Cheri Huber's all-time bestseller, *There Is Nothing Wrong with You*, published in 1993. Over the years, many "There Is Nothing Wrong With You" retreats have been filled by those inspired by the book to look more deeply into how we can free ourselves from the ravages of conditioning and self-hate.
ISBN 0-9710309-7-9

What You Practice Is What You Have further exposes the antics of conditioning and self-hate. Awareness practice tools, developed over the years by Cheri and the monks at the Zen Monastery Peace Center, are included.
ISBN 0-9710309-0-1